GIFTS FROM GARRETT

GIFTS FROM GARRETT

A Story of Love & Awakening

DANA SMITH

TYGAR PRESS

Tygar Press
P.O. Box 672
Bend, Oregon 97709-0672

Cover art and design by Angela Schular

For information about special discounts for bulk purchases or to book an event, please contact the publisher at info@tygarpess.com.

The names of some individuals in this book have been changed.

Published in the United States by Tygar Press

ISBN 978-0-9910973-0-2
ISBN 978-0-9910973-1-9 (ebook)

For my boys, Garrett and Ryan.

To every heart that longs for connection and peace.

Contents

Contents

"Mom, I know the cure for AIDS."
"What is it?"
"Love."

Foreword

Gifts from Garrett is actually a Gift from God, with Garrett and through Dana. I have been blessed to receive this gift a "little early," which of course, came at the perfect time for me. As gifts from God always do... right on time. Divine Time...

I have no doubt, and really neither do you, if this book has "found" its way into your life, that in receiving the gifts this beautiful book has to give, you will remember much of what you may have forgotten in your struggle, that absolutely ALL is Well... No matter what... And, when you begin to open again to the knowing that has always been with you, even if at this time it seems impossible to fathom, you will begin to know Peace again. True peace. The kind of peace that can only come from remembering God - and in turn, remembering who we Truly are...

A quote is on my desk, author "unknown": "Peace. It does not mean to be in a place where there is no noise, trouble or hard work. It means to be in the midst of those things and still be calm in your heart." For me, I know that the "unknown" part of this is God. And through Dana's beautiful book, I was able to be reminded of this as I was experiencing my own personal grief, although not as a result of a loved one's passing...

The gifts from Garrett and Dana are far-reaching, in that grief is really the forgetting of who we are - and no matter what external circumstances are occurring in our life at the moment, if we are experiencing sadness, fear or grief of any kind, it is only because we have forgotten our connection with Spirit, and in turn, our True Self. It seems simple. And it really is. Although I have discovered that simple does not mean the process of remembering is "easy," until it is...

Whatever you are experiencing in your life right now, please know that it is absolutely perfect. In every way. Even when it feels like there is no way in this world that could be true. Actually, the only way is to look beyond "this world," or what (we sometimes think) we can only see in this world, in order to know. If "looking beyond" seems like a stretch for you, then simply have the willingness to be open to "looking beyond" what your 5 senses can interpret. And if this willingness brings up fear in you from what you have been taught or "told," have the courage (with God) to ask yourself the Truth. Because I believe, with all my heart, that we each have the Truth within us, and we learn to trust our Truth/God, when we let go of all of our limiting beliefs. What do you think or believe? Is God Love or fear? Does God want us to live a closed-off, limited life, or an open, beautiful, all-knowing and giving life?

I am eternally thankful for Dana's presence and inspiration in my life. Her love, friendship, guidance, support and most-of-all, her sense of Peace, have been life-giving to me. She remembered True Peace through an experience that most of us would deem as the greatest loss we could ever experience on this Earth. Her greatest gift to me has been in the way she LIVES her life. And, when you know something so beautiful, with all of your heart, you really just want to share it... And so she is...

In Love,

Keely Shay

Acknowledgments

It is with all the love in my heart that I thank my beautiful son Garrett Kyle for his love and encouragement, in both his physical and nonphysical forms. He is the inspiration that brought this book to fruition. I also thank my beautiful son Ryan Miller for his love and understanding while *I've been working on my book*, and for choosing me as his mom and just being Ryan.

To my parents, Walt and Jeanette Smith, for always being in my corner with love, during all my ups and downs, the many moves, dog walks, caring for grandsons; whenever they receive a call, they show up and have shown me the gift of family and being a parent. To my brother, Craig Smith; sister, Lisa Cordero; and niece, Brittany Stipe; for their love, support, and the laughs and joys along life's path.

Keely Shay, my dear friend and angel. Her generosity, love, and giving nature is unmatched. I'm honored that she was inspired to write the beautiful Foreword of this book. Thank you Keely for the love you share we are all better for it.

To my earth angel friends Nina Durfee, Anna Goldsworthy, Angie Studer, Paula Thalmann, Roxanne Garner, and Julie Ouelette. Each of you has provided me deep heartfelt friendship that I treasure. Thank you for love, compassion, wisdom, and humor while I've tried to figure it out.

To the kids with whom I grieved—John Karp Evans, Willie Sloop, Jesse Chulay, Zach Nance, Aaron Laub, Phil Bestak, Emilee Lee, Lauren Sutton, Kelly Nettle, Brian Hanson, Chris Anton, Kelcey Costanzo, and Joe Escobar—and who have now grown up and become my friends. Thank you for your friendship with Garrett, Ryan, and me. I love you.

To those who invested time and energy in Garrett's vision of Garrett's Space: John Karp Evans, Dana Lough, Amy Kyle, and Laurey Maslyk.

Thank you to the talented Angela Schuler for the use of her beautiful butterfly for the cover of this book. Her generous spirit brought the yellow and black butterfly vision for the book cover to reality. A lovely example of the everyday connections that bring an artist who paints butterflies in Traverse City, Michigan, to a first-time author in Bend, Oregon.

I thank God and the many angels who have been with me all along. Some are mentioned in this book, and some are not, but I love and appreciate all for their contribution in helping me become more of my authentic self.

Prologue

Just when the caterpillar thought the world was over, it became a butterfly…
— English Proverb

Although there were signs along the way, I did not think my son Garrett would leave this physical world before me. I learned that he was hit by a train and was found hours later on the tracks. The devastation and despair was so overwhelming, I found that I couldn't stay in my body. I would go into this strange state of being *here* but not being *here*, it is difficult to describe. For a while, it was the only way I could cope with my new reality.

As more details came forward, so did more curiosity as to what had happened. Was he alone? Was there foul play? I soon realized that continuing to question "how" Garrett had passed, hiring a detective, or seeking *justice*, would only prolong my agony. Nothing would change the fact that Garrett was no longer in his body and all I wanted was Garrett back. I also began to understand although I wanted Garrett here with me, this didn't mean that something had *gone wrong*. I think the mystery in not knowing any details surrounding Garrett's transition was a gift in that it gave me the opportunity to advance my spiritual stamina.

For most of my life I have had a sense that there was *something more* I was supposed to do. Throughout my life, I had often paid attention and at the same time ignored my intuition, not really wanting to fully accept and embrace it. In the acceptance, there would be a responsibility that I wasn't ready to take on; I had fear of what others would think.

It wasn't until Garrett passed, my heart shattering event, that my path in life became obvious. I fully embraced all that I am and the world of the unseen. I am not only referring to loved ones in nonphysical, although this has been a beautiful gift in my life. I am also referring to the world of unseen love and grace that surrounds and is within us. My desire to stay connected to Garrett after his transition was stronger than my fears. I began to focus completely on connection with Garrett and with my deeper connection and knowing, and the opinions of others were becoming less of a factor.

There was something inside that I couldn't ignore, something bigger than me and I knew that I had to share our story. Initially, I thought this was going to be a book about Garrett, but it evolved in to much more. The last thing I wanted to do after Garrett passed was share my personal life with the world. I have always preferred to be behind the scenes, while Garrett enjoyed the spotlight. I am thankful for the time I had with Garrett while he was in his body, as we truly lived life to the fullest. One of the greatest blessings in my life is the gift of being Garrett's mother. Another, is learning our relationship is eternal.

Garrett has been with me every step while I've moved through my grief and as I wrote this book. We hope our story brings comfort to your heart, helps you embrace the light that shines within you and ultimately, helps you know peace.

Introduction

Grief is perhaps an unknown territory for you.
You might feel both helpless and hopeless without a sense of
a map for the journey. Confusion is the hallmark of a transition.
To rebuild both your inner and outer world is a major project.
— Ann Grant

When a loved one has left his or her body, those left behind can feel unspeakable grief. That was me, when my beautiful son Garrett unexpectedly passed at the age of nineteen.

From the physical perspective, I couldn't understand why a nineteen-year-old so full of life would suddenly pass in what was deemed to be an accident. At the time, I could not come to grips with this scenario or the endless tormenting thoughts that ran through my mind. I felt that my body, my entire being, was enveloped in despair. It was the most painful place I've ever been. Nothing I had felt before compared to the agony I felt when I looked at my new reality, the reality that my son was no longer in his body. I wanted to leave; I didn't want to be here anymore. It was too much to bear. At times I felt as if I were going crazy. I felt disconnected from myself, from God. I felt like I was in an abyss.

My perception had to change completely if I were to ever feel peace and rediscover the grace that surrounds us all. I had to look beyond the physical world. My journey to peace took me to depths within that I did not know existed; it led me to a spiritual awakening. I came to know that I am here to share my path of awakening that occurred as I transformed my grief and my way of *being*. It became clear to me that Garrett's passing was (and is) an agreement that he and I share. He would transition so that I would have the experience and would be able to share what I learned with others, with you.

I now know that Garrett's transition was a great gift of love from Garrett to all who love him, and he is loved by many. Had Garrett not transitioned, I never would have discovered the depth of my Soul, experienced the intensity of love, and the knowledge that relationships are eternal. Not just wanting to believe it's true, but *knowing* it's true, with every fiber of my being. Everything that has happened, every event, was given to me to awaken and embrace my spirituality.

When Garrett passed, I began to look at who we are and ultimately dispelled the notion that we die. We do leave our bodies, but we do not die. I've come to know that what most think of as extraordinary is, in truth, *ordinary*.

Knowing this is a game changer; it changes everything about life. Because of this knowing, I am able to feel the presence of my son, who is often with me. We have become closer than ever. Our love is deeper and stronger than the day he transitioned.

There are some basic core beliefs I have come to know and will share them here to clarify the context of my perspective:

- Whatever name you choose—God, Life Force, Spirit, the Divine, the Universe—doesn't make mistakes.
- Quantum physics tells us we are Conscious energy.
- The Soul, Higher Self, Inner Being—is all the same and is the essence of who we are.
- Since our Soul or our Consciousness does not die, I use the words pass or transition. These words more accurately express what happens when one leaves the body. The Consciousness passes through, or transitions, out of the body.
- There are no accidents; nothing is random.
- There is great purpose in everything that happens.
- We have pre-birth agreements with our loved ones.
- There is Divine timing and order when we come into our bodies and when we leave them.

These are my beliefs. I had to keep reminding myself of them as I was reevaluating the beliefs I was taught by my family and by Western culture. I discovered what I had been taught wasn't really what I believed at all. As I worked through my grief process, I tested my old beliefs, realized what beliefs were no longer true for me, recognized what was true for me, and began to live the new ones. I had to work diligently to remind myself of my true beliefs; I could not fall back into the old-pattern responses that I didn't even believe.

I hope, with all my heart, my story will help you to transform your grief into a beautiful spiritual awakening and continued awareness of your connection with your loved one.

If you're like I was, you've felt enough pain and are ready to surrender, to feel peace.

I've come to know there are no accidents and that coincidences are meant to happen; events are meant to perfectly coincide. As you've found this book in your hands, you can be sure your loved one has helped you to find the answers and the peace you desire.

Much Love,

Dana

Chapter One

Growing Up

Everything Flows
—Lao-tzu

Have you ever looked at your life in retrospect and recognized a pivotal moment? I was born in Tacoma, Washington, and lived with my parents, Jeanette and Dick, and my sister, Lisa, who is five years older than me. My father was a construction foreman who specialized in building bridges. In 1966 we were living in Portland, Oregon, while my father was working on a bridge project. He drove a 1966 Fastback Mustang that he loved. My sister and I would look forward to his coming home from work; it was a ritual. I was filled with anticipation and excitement to see him at the end of the day. Nineteen sixty-six turned out to be a pivotal year for my family.

My sister and I waited as usual for our father to return home from work, but he was late, so my mom let us stay up past our bedtime. He still hadn't come home, and she finally put us to bed. We shared a bedroom and had been in bed only long enough for my sister to fall asleep when I heard a knock and my mother open the door. I thought it must be him, that he must finally be home. But it wasn't my father; it was the neighbor. I heard him tell my mother there was a car accident, that my father was dead. My mother asked if he was sure it was him, and then I heard my mother sobbing. I woke my sister and told her, "Daddy's dead." She didn't believe me at first, so I told her to listen to Mom. We could both hear our mother crying. Then we both began to cry, too. Even though I was only four, I knew I wouldn't see my father again. Somehow, I understood.

Later, I learned that he was driving on his way home from work on the freeway. It was raining hard. It was dark, and the Mustang that he loved hydroplaned. He was not wearing a seatbelt and was thrown from the car.

Our entire family came for the funeral: my mother's family from Tacoma, Washington, and my father's large family from the Bay Area. My mother wanted me to remember my father alive and didn't want me to be traumatized by a funeral, which meant I wasn't allowed to attend the funeral. Although now I understand her thinking, at the time I did not understand. I adored my father. I felt left out, especially when my older sister was allowed to attend.

Shortly after his funeral in Portland, we took a trip to Santa Clara, California, and stayed with my grandmother. We visited the grave where my father was buried. Because my father was from a large family, many of them were around during this time, and I felt safe. It was the first time I remember seeing my grandmother. There was a good feeling with her, and I liked being around my family. My mother told me years later that my father's family wanted her to move to California and be near them, and her family wanted her to move back to Washington to be near them. She decided to stay in Portland to rebuild her life and raise my sister and me. I admire her for her strength and independence during this time.

Life was emotional for a while. My mother cried often, and when I saw her I would comfort her by giving her a hug. I didn't like seeing my mother sad. When I was an adult, my mother told me that I had said to her, "I wish I had a spray and could spray Daddy back." She also shared after his passing her vivid dreams of my father showing her his new home. In those days, there was no grief counseling or bereavement groups. We just moved forward without the emotional support that is available now.

It was my mom, my sister, and me for a while. A couple years later, my mother married a wonderful man, Walt, who has been an amazing father to me since I was six years old.

My mom had another baby—my brother, Craig. I was thrilled; I adored him. We were an average middle-class family living in Gresham, a small suburb east of Portland. My father Walt was a firefighter, and my mother worked part time in retail.

As a child I wanted to be good because I adored my parents. I had good friends, liked school, and I've always loved to learn. I took dance classes, participated in gymnastics, and was a high school football cheerleader. I was both a bit of an introvert and extrovert, which hasn't changed. While I enjoy being with others, my alone time is important to me. When I got into high school, I had a strong desire for independence. This caused friction with my mother, which is ironic since I believe I got this from her DNA. My dad and I, on the other hand, have always gotten along.

Neither of my parents were religious or spiritual. While growing up I always thought my dad was an atheist, it wasn't until recently I learned he is agnostic. I'm not sure why but when I was ten, my mother decided I should go to church. She had made an arrangement with my friend's parents to take me to church on Sundays. She didn't ask me if I wanted to go; she simply told me I was going. As an obedient child, I didn't question her, although I didn't particularly want to go. It was a local Christian church that I attended for six years. Once I started going, I enjoyed it but would have preferred to attend with my own family.

Although I felt love for God, I feared not believing in God. I was afraid to do anything wrong, that if I didn't believe in Jesus I would go to hell. I spent many nights worried about this. I did believe that Jesus existed, but I questioned my motives. Did I believe because I was afraid not to, or because I really knew? I was sure God would know my true motive when the time came. There were a few key messages that I was taught in church that seemed contradictory to me. I never questioned these things to others, although they didn't feel right to me.

I didn't understand how Jesus and God could be so loving and yet not let people who might never have heard about them go to hell, or send anyone there. The dying for our sins message didn't make sense to me either. This seemed to contradict his teachings. Jesus is the son of God, I believed, but what about the rest of us—aren't we too? These were things that didn't seem to add up.

During my elementary school years, I would see sparkling colors of light in front of me and near me. At the time I didn't know what this was, but I never questioned it. I just saw it from time to time. I never asked anyone else if they saw it. The sparkling light never bothered me; instead, it comforted me. It was natural to see, like the chalkboard on the classroom wall.

I recall always having a sense about others. If they were lying to me, I could feel it. Emotions people had that they internalized, I could feel. I was using more advanced senses at the time and didn't realize it. It was natural, just like hearing. Seeing the sparkling light was normal, so I never thought it was strange or unique. Over time, the sparkling light went away, and I didn't even notice that I wasn't seeing it any longer; however, the other senses stayed with me.

When I was in the eighth grade, I participated in the confirmation program at our church. After graduating from confirmation, the church held a baptismal for those who were confirmed and anyone in the congregation. I decided to get baptized as the completion of the process of confirmation. I wasn't prepared for the experience that I had. Until then, I felt that God was outside of me. I prayed and studied the Bible. It didn't occur to me that I could feel God until I was baptized. As I was baptized, I could feel this energy throughout my body, a sort of tingling inside me. It was nothing that I remember ever being discussed at church or during preparation for baptism. Although I wasn't sure exactly what I was experiencing, I did know it was something special, some sort of connection. It felt wonderful.

I never spoke to anyone about it. Before long, it left my everyday thoughts. Looking back, I believe the reason I didn't speak about this was that those around me didn't seem to have the same experience. If my peers in confirmation class had had a similar experience, they did not share it with me. Certainly, I couldn't talk to anyone in my family about my experience since no one talked about God or spirituality. I let the outside dictate to me and ignored my first strong feeling of connection to the Divine.

Independence and freedom were very important to me as a teenager. I couldn't wait to get a car, which meant getting a job to pay for it. At fifteen, I got my first job, taking orders at a local pizza restaurant. I answered an ad in the paper, and my mom took me to my interview. I was hired on the spot, and I was thrilled. I saved my money and bought my first car when I was sixteen. I have always been a goal-oriented person. Even now, it's fun to set an intention and then begin the process of achieving it.

When I was seventeen, I had a fake ID and was a bit of a party girl. I loved to dance and frequented places I was too young to attend.

While I was in high school, the country seemed to turn its attention on us. Geologists had been watching Mt. St. Helens and warning that volcanic activity would lead to a large eruption. Then, on May 18, 1980, Mt. St. Helens erupted as predicted. It was a big deal. Portland is about fifty miles from the mountain. The volcanic ash from the explosion seemed to be everywhere. The eruption destroyed the immediate area, and those who didn't evacuate did not survive the blast. We were far enough away that we were safe, but it was the first experience I'd had with a disaster.

Mine were typical teenage years. I could not wait to graduate from high school. I was ready to get on with my life even though I had no clear direction about what I wanted to do after graduation. A long-term view of my life had not occurred to me. I liked to travel and thought I might become a flight attendant. Neither of my parents attended college, and the thought of going to a four-year college didn't occur to me as an option. It was never on the table, never discussed in my family. Moreover, direction and guidance in this area were never provided. I tried different things: I attended community college, beauty school, and travel school, but I wasn't passionate about any of these. There was an underlying notion that I would get married and have a family, although that wasn't a big dream of mine at the time.

CHAPTER TWO

Marrying Kevin

If you begin to understand what you are without trying to change it, then what you are undergoes a transformation.
—Krishnamurti

I met Kevin Kyle in the summer after I graduated from high school. Kevin was thirteen years my senior. We met at a local hot-spot bar; he was charming, fun, and had a good sense of humor. We moved in together about nine months after we met, but I found myself unprepared for this kind of relationship. My mother had cleaned my room for me until I moved in with Kevin. I had no tools for interpersonal skills in a serious relationship, and he didn't either. This resulted in regular arguments, even though this was not what my parents modeled in their marriage.

Yet, Kevin seemed to love me, and he told me so often. He wrote poetry for me, was thoughtful, made dinners, and had bubble baths waiting for me when I came home from work. He had a very sweet side. He asked me almost every day to marry him. I wondered, *Could I live the rest of my life with this man?* And then one day he asked, and I said, "Yes."

Even though I had this nagging feeling I shouldn't marry him, I did. We eloped and married in Lake Tahoe, California, within a year of meeting each other. I had never been to Lake Tahoe and fell in love with the area. I was home. The beauty was overwhelming; it literally took my breath away. Tahoe had a special energy. I could feel it. I had always thought myself more of a city person until I arrived in Tahoe.

Kevin had a two-year-old son from a previous marriage. Even though my parents were probably a bit dismayed about the whole thing, it had always been their way to support me no matter what choice I had made. Wisely, they embraced the situation. Kevin's parents, who were Catholic, were not pleased about our getting married and also not pleased that he and his first wife divorced.

During our marriage, I was still growing up and only beginning to figure out who I was. It was a tumultuous relationship, one in which I was never really happy. Kevin couldn't have been happy either. The direction of my life was based on what I thought I should do, which was to get married and have a family. I never really asked myself if I was in love with him, I focused on his love for me. I ignored what I needed. At nineteen, I didn't know who I was, or what kind of marriage I wanted. From the outside, which is where I was living, we had a good life in many ways. We were healthy, living a middle-class lifestyle, and we had close friends and family. Although on the inside I was miserable, it became my normal.

My work was work. I worked just to earn a paycheck. That's what I thought work was about. At that time in my life my work was not about doing something I enjoyed; rather, it was about earning a living. I had a variety of office jobs: working for attorneys, working as a consultant, and working for a Fortune 500 company in high technology. I always enjoyed the relationships with my coworkers and the experience gained in business, but I never felt fulfilled. I never felt that I fully belonged. I simply didn't have a passion for the corporate world. At the time, I don't think I realized that it was possible to be passionate about work. Work was more to be endured, a means to finance a lifestyle, living Friday at five through Sunday evening, which was a feeling shared by everyone else I knew.

I did not know what I really wanted to do. I remember praying all the time, asking for help. I felt lost; I was going through the motions of what I thought I should do. When I struggled, I felt as if my problems were not big enough for God, that God didn't have time for my problems. But now I know that God was always there waiting for me. After five years of marriage, I had a strong desire for a baby. I remember when the timing just felt right. As I look back on it now, I think it was a spiritual nudge.

My first child, Garrett, was born three days before my twenty-fifth birthday. My father and I have the same birthday, and we were hoping he would be born on our birthday—but he arrived on his own day. I couldn't wait for Garrett to arrive. It was a big deal; he was the first grandchild on my side of the family.

From the moment I met Garrett in his physical form, I felt an undeniable spiritual connection, which I didn't expect. I clearly remember the evening he was born, watching him in his little bed at the hospital. He was alert, looking around at everything. Even then he was curious. When he and I were all alone in the hospital room, it was around midnight. I was holding him, taking it all in, marveling that he was here and how beautiful he was. While I was in this place of wonder, I felt a strong energy fill the room; it was palpable. It's hard to find words to describe it. The best way for me to describe this is the feeling it gave, which was love. It felt as if it was a part of Garrett. I knew that his energy connected us, similar to the energy I felt when I was baptized, but this energy actually filled the room. I felt a tingling inside me. It would be many years later, in a profound moment, when I would feel this energy again.

When Garrett was four months old, I knew I wanted a divorce. Things between Kevin and I were not good. Over the years we had left our problems unresolved, so they just kept getting bigger. We argued tirelessly over the same things and got nowhere. There was a monotony and a drudgery that set in to my life. I take responsibility for my part in our marriage not working out. I shouldn't have been surprised things weren't a whole lot different after we were married than before. I was young when we married; I didn't have the foresight that things wouldn't change. There were issues that felt insurmountable to me, and I was changing. Kevin didn't like that I was growing up.

He was, in my view, addicted to marijuana. For years I told him it wasn't something I wanted in our household, especially with a family. He said he wouldn't smoke and continued to lie to me about it. I didn't understand his addiction and why he was not willing to stop. His temper was short and he was moody, and I'm sure his drug use influenced his temperament. He was also controlling, a behavior that seemed to escalate over the years. The more I tried to grow, the more insecure he became—or, more likely, the more I noticed his insecurities. He didn't like my having any outside-the-house activities; even my taking a needlepoint class was an argument. I wanted to learn and grow, and Kevin wanted to keep me down. He constantly scrutinized my time. He called my work regularly at five to make sure I was on my way home. I was extremely unhappy and did not have the tools at the time to know how to change my situation. I felt guilty, after having this little boy, for wanting to break up his family. I told myself I could stick it out.

We tried marriage counseling. By that time, however, I had already checked out. I didn't have the energy for it. I was frustrated and angry by the drug use. It was not what I wanted in my life or in Garrett's life.

In retrospect, I was unhappy because I was making choices that did not reflect who I was, and it made me miserable. I kept most of my feelings hidden from others and, at times, myself. I chose to stay in a marriage that was destructive for both of us. I thought it was what I should do. I didn't have the capacity at the time to look within and discover who I was and what type of career I really wanted. Other than being a mother to a son I adored, there was no other area in my life that I was living authentically.

Garrett's father and I were married for nine years. We divorced when Garrett was four. At the suggestion of a marriage counselor, we decided during our separation that Garrett would stay in the house, and Kevin and I would rotate in and out every other week. This way, Garrett's routine wouldn't be disrupted. I stayed with my parents the week that I was away from Garrett. I began running during this time, and it helped tremendously to relieve the stress.

The living situation was a recipe for disaster. I became the every-other-week maid and yard keeper at the house. I would leave it clean and come home to a mess. I became even more infuriated when Kevin's new girlfriend began staying in our home during his week with Garrett. I didn't care if Kevin was seeing someone; I just didn't feel it was appropriate to bring someone into our home while Garrett was experiencing this change. We had set up the arrangement with the intent that this would support Garrett's well-being. Bringing another person into the home was not a decision, from my perspective, that supported Garrett's well-being. The fact that Kevin wanted joint custody and I wanted full custody made matters even worse.

In hindsight the living situation was a blessing. As I rotated in and out of the house, I learned what it's like to rotate between homes. For those few months, I felt like I had no home. It was also clear that Kevin and I could not get on the same page as to decisions regarding Garrett. I was not willing to subject Garrett to rotating households after having lived this way myself. My lawyer informed me that judges don't really like joint custody because people with it tend to end up back in court. We met with a psychologist individually and with Garrett, and she recommended full custody with me. At the eleventh hour before court, Kevin decided to let it go, and I was awarded full custody of Garrett.

Chapter Three

Personal Growth

Listen to your heart. It knows all things.
—Paulo Coelho, The Alchemist

My marriage taught me to always be true to myself. Once we split up, I was happy for the first time in years. A whole new world opened up. I was giddy about life; a weight was lifted from my shoulders; and I could feel a new lightness in my body. I had released myself from my own prison.

While our house was for sale, Garrett and I moved in with my parents for about four months. I bought a cute two-bedroom condo in West Linn, an area twenty minutes south of Portland. Although it was a bit of a commute to work downtown, it was worth living in a beautiful area known as one of the best school districts in the state.

At this time, I experienced remarkable personal growth. Soon after our separation, a colleague invited me to run on our company's Hood to Coast team. It was a twelve-person, 195-mile relay run that began at Timberline Lodge on Mt. Hood and ended in Seaside, Oregon. Training for and participating in this event was huge in getting me back on track with myself. Running is meditative for me. I didn't realize this at the time. All I knew was that I felt good when I ran. I had never done this before. Doing a new activity that was healthy and calming gave me confidence and a new awareness about myself. If I could do this race, I could do anything. It was symbolic for me; my newfound me.

I began to notice my intuitive connection with others. It was as if a cloud had lifted from me, or, as I know now, by feeling so much better, I raised my vibration level. I became aware of my intuitive abilities, particularly with those to whom I was close. I knew when they were thinking of me, when they were going to call me. Although I was aware of this, I didn't give it much thought.

My corporate career was in high technology under the sales, marketing, and public relations umbrellas. For a while I spent a significant amount of time planning and executing elaborate, high-profile events. While there were aspects that were fun and creative, it was extremely stressful with constant deadlines and follow-ups, hiring talent and finding the perfect venues. After one large event in particular, I was in an elevator with some of my peers. They shared with me how much they enjoyed the event and were complimentary. While I was pleased and appreciated their feedback, I couldn't help but think, *In ten years, who is going to remember this?* While it was a success in that the goals were achieved after all my hard work, I felt empty.

My manager, who was the director of public affairs, told me she had a friend who was finishing her degree at Marylhurst University, a local liberal arts university that specializes in educating working adults. She encouraged me to go to school and get my degree. I did my research and decided to go back to school. I spent the next three years working, going to school full time, and raising Garrett. It was one of the best times in my life. I finally felt like me again. I was excited about life, about learning, and little Garrett was sweet and supportive. Although I didn't know it at the time, this is when I began my spiritual path. I'm grateful to my manager and for her encouragement and support. Going back to school changed my life in ways I could never have imagined.

Even though the divorce and custody for Garrett was a stressful process, things fell into place. When I began school at Marylhurst, I felt like I was home. Everything about being at school felt right. I became more self-aware. As I delved into my courses, which I was enjoying, I began feeling a weight on my shoulders. I literally felt as if I were being weighed down. I couldn't figure it out. Something was off, and after feeling good since my divorce I wanted to identify what it was and get back on track.

One afternoon I met with one of my favorite professors, and I shared with her the feeling I was experiencing. I was a bit emotional but wasn't sure why. Was this because I was going to school full time, working full time, and raising Garrett on my own? Did I simply have a lot on my plate? She listened to my story, and during our discussion I realized there was another change coming into view. In many of the classes I was taking, I was discovering more about me. My discomfort wasn't due to my heavy schedule; it was the career direction in which I was headed that was troubling me. I decided to change my degree program. I wasn't sure where it would lead, but I felt the immediate relief once I had made the choice to make a change. It would have been more logical to stay in the communications program, my company would have continued to pay for my tuition. I chose to study human sciences without the financial support of my company. I didn't care about the money. It was more important that I felt the relief and the sense that I was on the right path. It was an exciting time for me and the first time I felt truly happy in my adult life. Prior to my divorce, I was used to a way of life and went along with it because I did not know it could be different. Later I learned that when your energy shifts, things around you begin to change. This is exactly what I was experiencing, and I enjoyed it fully. Once I changed my energy, new doors and opportunities opened.

Garrett, my beautiful blond-haired, blue-eyed boy, was charismatic even as a child. He had a special charm. He was curious and loved fun and adventure. He was also a loving, thoughtful boy; he picked daisies for me and always wanted to give me gifts. One of our favorite things to do on Friday nights was to lie in bed, eat Häagen-Dazs Bars, and watch *Nick at Nite*.

One spring break, Garrett flew to Texas to visit my parents and returned on his ninth birthday. Even though Garrett was quite capable, and it was pre-9/11, I was nervous about his traveling on a plane with a layover all by himself. I was excited and relieved when he returned. I had missed him while he was away and eagerly waited at the gate for Garrett's plane to arrive. As he came through the gate, he was beaming. The flight attendant told me he had offered to help them on the plane. They appreciated his offer and gave him the task of collecting the garbage for them. In return they gave him an extra food treat. The flight attendants and even a few passengers shared high praises for Garrett with me. Garrett had told them it was his birthday, so during the flight the passengers on the plane sang *Happy Birthday* to him. He loved it, but that was Garrett helping and making connections.

Although it was his birthday, he had two gifts for me which he had won at an arcade: a silver necklace with white and black beads and a pink plastic ring. I still wear both pieces of jewelry. When I wore the ring to work, I would get comments about it and loved telling people it was a gift from my son.

While at Marylhurst, I had taken several transformative classes, one weekend class in particular that touched something deep and profound inside me. We were learning transformational work, and the class was discussing what would be worse than death, or what would be more painful or scary than dying. Immediately, my emotion swelled within, and I held back tears as my answer to this question came quite easily: it would be if Garrett died. That *thought* left a dark, terrifying, empty feeling within me. It was the feeling of having no connection with him, of being completely cut off from each other. Harboring the thought was unbearable. Garrett was nine-years-old at the time, and for an entire year I worried. I feared something would happen to him. I just couldn't seem to shake this fear; the thought was constantly on my mind. After about a year, this fear finally subsided.

One of my degree requirements was an internship. I chose to do this at a place called The Dougy Center, located in Portland, Oregon. The Dougy Center is known internationally for the work they do with grieving children. One of the counselors at The Dougy Center taught a class I had taken at the university. I became interested in learning more about what they did and wanted to work with children.

The Dougy Center facility is a converted house, which provides a warm, comfortable environment to process grief. The focus is on children who have had someone close to them pass. The Dougy Center is a nonprofit and funded by donations. They don't require any family to pay.

I knew that volunteers were required to undergo intensive training before working with the families, but I had no idea volunteers were required to share their own grief experiences. It didn't occur to me before the training that the volunteers would have this connection. I was here for my internship, right? My father's passing had been so long ago, it wasn't in my day-to-day consciousness. Every volunteer had the traumatic experience of a loved one leaving. Why did this surprise me? We were a diverse group of all ages and backgrounds. The circumstances of each volunteer were wide ranging, from the passing of parents and children to suicides, illness, accidents, and murder.

This was the first time I was in a group space where no one judged anyone. I empathized with my peers. I could see and feel the pain and anguish as my peers shared their stories, their experiences with grief. They were raw and they were real. There was compassion and a healing power of bearing witness as someone speaks his or her story.

I rarely shared my father's car crash with anyone or my feelings about it. I was never asked, and my emotions were buried over years. I didn't even know how I felt until I started speaking my experience. I felt my emotion release through tears as I shared my experience of my dad's passing. I missed him, I would have loved to have known him, and wished that I could remember more moments with him. Verbalizing my feelings and acknowledging what had happened was a release. I let go of emotions I didn't realize I carried, which surprised me because I was at peace with my father's passing. Although I would have liked to have known him, I didn't live in what might have been. I'm sure it made all the difference that I'd had another wonderful father who was in my life from a young age.

The children are placed in groups by age, with a professional staff member and trained volunteers. The parents stay together as a group with trained volunteer facilitators. My internship included working with all ages—children, teens, and adults. I loved being with all of them. The children met in a large room filled with stuffed teddy bears and unlit white candles in the middle of the room. When the children came in, they would each select from a large inventory a teddy bear to hold, and the volunteers would sit in a circle around the candles with the children. As we went around the room, each child would share with the group who had passed in their life and light a candle for that person. It was lovely, heartwarming, and sometimes heartbreaking. These children were so sweet, and they understood why they were there. I don't remember any of the smaller children crying for their loved ones during their groups. Except for the teddy bears, the teens started the same way as the younger children, and they shed tears.

In the adult group, there were many tears shed. Here, I noticed something interesting. As a volunteer I appreciated that we were included in all the circles. After all, it was an inclusive environment; everyone was in it together. We were all navigating our way. It wasn't about having an answer or telling people what they should do, but rather about listening and holding a safe space and honoring people's place in their process. With the children it was play therapy and all kinds of options for play—arts and crafts, toys, games, the volcano room where they could punch bags, and an outdoor play area, every activity imaginable.

After each group had left, the volunteers would meet with a counselor from The Dougy Center. We would debrief together to address anything we would like to clear after our time with the families.

This internship lasted for a year. It was one of the best experiences I've ever had, yet another place where I felt at home. It confirmed that I did not want to continue a career in the corporate world. There was something more, deeper; heart work was calling me.

Chapter Four

Lake Tahoe

Follow your bliss.
—Joseph Campbell

I've always been rather goal oriented, more interested in getting to the place I want to be rather than enjoying the journey to get there, mostly looking forward rather than being present in the now. As I was finishing up with school, the company I was working for had just completed a merger, and there were rumors that people were going to be losing their jobs. This felt like a perfect opportunity. I was on the fast track to completing my four-year degree in a little less than three years. Completing my degree and the possibility of being packaged out of my position would coincide. I was excited to move forward in a new direction with my life. When it looked as if my position at work was going to be eliminated, I received a clear vision of living in Lake Tahoe.

Since my first visit to Lake Tahoe when Kevin and I were married, I dreamt of living there someday. Previously, the only way I could fathom this dream coming to fruition would be at my retirement in the distant future. When I'm in Lake Tahoe, a wave of emotion washes over me. I have a strong physical and emotional connection with the land. I feel as if I'm in a magnificent cathedral. The enormous, near-pristine sapphire lake surrounded by the Sierra Mountain Range, the large pine trees dotting the landscape, and the clean, crisp, pine-scented air. When I'm there I feel like I'm in church all the time. The Sierra Mountains and the lake energy combined always take my breath away. Whenever I drive up the hill to the lake, my body tingles; the energy radiates; and it always uplifts me. It's as if I'm coming home, even though I had only visited a handful of times. Mark Twain described it best:

> As it lay there with the shadows of the mountains brilliantly photographed upon its still surface I thought it must surely be the fairest picture the whole earth affords.

Here is another of Twain's descriptions:

> The air up there in the clouds is very pure and fine, bracing and delicious. And why shouldn't it be?—it is the same the angels breathe.

After receiving my vision of living in Lake Tahoe, my perspective shifted. I realized I did not have to wait until I was ready to retire. I could move there at any time. Why wait until I retire? Why not live where I really want to live now? There was no reason not to go. School and work were coming to completion, and a new chapter in my life was beginning. The Universe not only showed me the way but was opening the door to a new life.

During the first few years after my divorce, Garrett was often disappointed by broken promises from Kevin. On many occasions, while Garrett was staying with his dad, he would call me late at night and ask me to come and pick him up. It broke my heart to tell him I couldn't come and get him, that he had to stay with his dad. Kevin would have been furious if he even knew Garrett called me; most certainly Garrett would have received the brunt of his anger. Instead, I would stay on the phone and talk to him and try to help him feel better. It was difficult to watch Kevin constantly emotionally hurt Garrett. It would be easier on Garrett, I thought, to miss his father rather than experience the constant emotional abuse. So, it was an easy decision to move out of state with Garrett. We agreed on a visitation schedule. Garrett would visit him often, which he did.

After I completed school, I sold my condo and followed my vision and my heart. Garrett and I moved to South Lake Tahoe, California. He was nine-years-old, and he was excited about the move.

Since my divorce, new opportunities and ideas kept opening up, and I was listening and following my heart every step of the way. It was exhilarating. My parents helped us move into a house I rented and stayed with us for a few weeks. After they left, I realized I was on my own in a completely new place, and I knew no one. There was a cold fear that ran through me as I thought, *I'm all alone*. I quickly realized the value of networking. In Tahoe I had no one to network with to find a job, which was a strange feeling since so much of my work life had been about networking. Leaving all my contacts in Portland, I started from scratch.

Just before my move, I had seen author Sarah Ban Breathnach on the *Oprah Winfrey Show*. They were discussing her book, *Simple Abundance: A Daybook of Comfort and Joy*. I bought the book and tried to follow it every day. At the very least, I would write down five things each day I was thankful to have in my life. It was easy and became fun thinking of what I was thankful for: living in Lake Tahoe, my beautiful son, our health, the home we found to rent, drinking coffee from my favorite cup. I'm certain this practice helped me to make my move and connect me to my first job in Tahoe.

I saw an ad in the paper and interviewed for a job in events. The interviewer had said, "You'd be perfect to work with a friend of mine." She referred me to him, and I met with him and he hired me on the spot to work for his cruise ship. This is how I met my future employer, whom I met while booking their corporate cruise. My next job, of course, was a better one. I accomplished this in two months.

My new job was in the high-technology arena working for a start-up software company. I figured I would continue my schooling at some point and get a master's degree. I still had a desire to change career fields. But first, I wanted to get my bearings in our new town.

I began working in sales doing administrative work, organizing events, and going to trade shows. It worked while I was getting assimilated in our new home. The people I worked with were a special group—very dedicated. Most of them had moved to the area for the company. Because they had moved their families from all over the country, off the beaten path of corporate America, they had a lot invested, which made it even more appealing. Being in a start-up reminded me of my time in the cellular industry when it first began. There is a buzz of excitement and because it was small, people got to know each other and their families. There were Friday night pizza get-togethers and many opportunities for social interaction.

Six months after moving to Tahoe, I bought my then dream home. When we first moved to Tahoe, Garrett wanted to get a black Labrador retriever, but we couldn't while we were renting a house. Now that we had our house, we adopted a two-year-old black Labrador retriever, BJ; we also adopted a cat, Casey, along with our cockapoo, Sammy.

The clear vision of our life I'd had while I was in school had been more than fulfilled. Our house was on an acre backing to forest with a rather large creek running through it. From our street, which was on a hill, there was a lake view. The kitchen window provided a partial view of the lake. On the main level were the kitchen, great room, and a bedroom, all facing the forest with the mountains and pine trees, with a large deck that ran the length of the house. Downstairs was the master, Garrett's room, a good-size storage room, and laundry. There was a large Jack and Jill bathroom that Garrett and I shared. In the middle was a large shower on one side and a large soaking tub with a window overlooking the forest. Off the master were stairs leading down to a large deck and another room we called the spa room, which had a hot tub and a sauna. The house was light and airy. While lying in my bed, I could see the sunrise from behind the mountains. I loved watching the sky turn from a purplish color to a beautiful pink before the sun fully rose. It was a spectacular show.

I looked forward to coming home from work and walking along the creek with Garrett, BJ, and Sammy in our backyard forest. Smelling the fresh pine and clear, crisp air, we were happy and my heart would sing. It was heaven.

Wearing his fishing hat and carrying his fishing pole and tackle box, Garrett would take BJ and go to the creek in our backyard and fish. In the winter, he would build jumps in the backyard and ride his snowboard down the hill and over them, with BJ following. It was an ideal setting for a nine-year-old boy.

Garrett and I spent time exploring the lake area and going on hikes. We made new friends. My life was completely transformed in just five years. It was better than I dreamed possible, and I loved it.

Our first winter in Tahoe, Garrett joined a ski program that was run by parent volunteers. Through this program we skied together every weekend during the season. This is one of my fondest memories from Garrett's childhood. We loved being on the mountain. Sharing our love of skiing was a joy, and so we spent many wonderful days together on the mountain. It wasn't long before he was down the mountain ahead of me. Garrett began snowboarding at the age of eleven and eventually joined the Foundation Team at Heavenly. He would snowboard at every available opportunity. Snowboarding remained a love of his for the rest of his life.

We were a small, close-knit family. My parents, brother, and sister came to see us often. Tahoe became the family gathering place. My niece, Brittany (my sister Lisa's daughter), was two years younger than Garrett, and they adored each other. She was more like a kid sister than a cousin. He loved to make her laugh. She spent several vacations with us.

Chapter Five

Life with Josh

The purpose of life is to live it, to reach out eagerly and without fear for newer and richer experience.
—Eleanor Roosevelt

When I started working, the sales organization was just beginning to grow. One of my duties was to coordinate travel arrangements for interviewees. One person in particular had everyone abuzz with his talent, and the executives were falling all over themselves to hire him. I first met Josh Miller over the phone, helping him get his flights coordinated for his interview at the corporate office. When he came into the office, I introduced myself. He was kind and gracious. He was hired immediately and at the time was living in the Midwest. Shortly after, he was hired. He managed the North American sales team, and I was his corporate inside sales contact.

Josh's schedule, being two hours ahead, worked out perfect for me. It allowed me to connect with him in the morning, on the early side my time, which gave me the opportunity to be home to get Garrett to the bus stop on my way to work. By the time I got to work, my day had already begun. I enjoyed working with him. He knew the work that needed to be done, and he had a good sense of humor. Before long, everyone wanted to work for him, even some of the developers. It was his leadership that drew people to him. He was a natural leader and attributed these skills to his previous marine training. I liked, respected, and appreciated the opportunity to learn from him. Within the first six months, he pulled in a huge sale on December 30. He saved the company on the numbers we would be reporting to investors. He was everyone's hero.

The following month, all the sales people came to the corporate office for an annual kickoff meeting. The entire team went out to dinner afterward. That evening Josh took me aside and told me that he had feelings for me. It was completely unexpected. He also married at nineteen and had been unhappy for many years. I told him I had lived that and had learned the most important thing in life is to be true to yourself. I also told him I wasn't interested in a married man. If he was unhappy, he needed to deal with his life and leave me out of it.

We didn't talk about it again and continued moving forward with work. A few months later, he called and told me he was separated, and the formal divorce process had begun. He wanted to start seeing me. When I asked him if he wanted to spend time alone to get his bearings, he said, "You are the person I've always pictured, and I've been so unhappy for so many years. I want to start my life now." He also told me when we first met in person and shook hands, he felt electricity all through his body. When he said all he wanted was to be with Garrett and me, he had me. We started dating. There wasn't anything about him that I didn't adore. He was smart, witty, and romantic. Plus, we were friends; we clicked; and our relationship was easy. We had the same values and beliefs. He liked learning and growing, too. He seemed to be everything I was looking for in a mate.

Two years after Garrett and I moved to Tahoe, Josh and I married. Garrett was eleven and happy with the marriage.

Josh moved into my home and, over time, our family grew. We got another dog, Chico, a black flat-coated retriever, a little terrier, Bucky, and a cat, Blackie. Financially, things were tight when we were first married. Josh had some significant debt that I wasn't aware of until after we were married. I wasn't thrilled to discover this, and he had been embarrassed to tell me. Having already experienced financial challenges from a divorceI knew that financial recovery can happen. Luckily, I had resources and was able and happy to help out with the majority of it.

Days before our wedding, Kevin's mother passed. Garrett wanted to go to Portland for the funeral, and Kevin told him he couldn't go, even though we offered to fly Garrett to Portland. Kevin told Garrett he wouldn't pick him up from the airport and take him to the funeral. Garrett was crushed. He badly wanted to be at the funeral for his grandmother.

The wedding party and family were already arriving at my house, and I didn't know how I could leave in the middle of it all. Josh stepped in and offered to fly with Garrett to Portland and take him to his grandmother's funeral. Just as he was about to make the plane reservations, Garrett decided not to go. When I asked him why he changed his mind, he told me that he thought his dad would be mad at him for coming. My heart broke for Garrett. There was nothing I could do to help, other than support him.

Josh came into our lives at a good time for Garrett. Garrett was happy when I married Josh. He was never one to be shy. He wanted to be the best man at our wedding and gave a beautiful toast he put together on his own, when he was only eleven years old. I had no idea that he was going to give one, but he brought down the house with his touching words. He shared that he was happy because his mom was so happy. I was proud and deeply touched by his loving words.

After Josh and I were married, even though he loved Kevin, Garrett began calling Josh, *Dad*. Kevin kept Garrett at a distance. Garrett had shared with me that there were times when he was afraid of Kevin. Something very few people knew about Garrett was that he was highly sensitive. A glance, strong words, or a certain tone would crush him. I could see it all over his face. He tried to hide it, but I knew. I knew my boy, and although he sometimes tried to be tough on the outside, I knew when something hurt him. He longed for a close relationship with Kevin. Garrett carried a wound in his heart his entire life from feelings of not being accepted by his father. My marrying Josh gave Garrett the opportunity for a father–son relationship that he longed to have.

During this time, both Josh and I had a change in work circumstances. I left the software company I had been working for a few months before we got married.

Josh had left the software company before I did. He had taken a position as general manager with a company that consulted to the automotive industry, so he was commuting to Detroit quite often. After he began working for this new company, he realized they hadn't been transparent in their portrayal of the business. Josh felt duped and was frustrated, angry, and stressed. The stress due to his work was penetrating all parts of our lives. He would spend hours sharing his frustrations, trying to resolve situations, but to no avail. The final straw came on what we called a beautiful bluebird day.

It had snowed the night before. The lake was a gorgeous, deep sapphire blue, the sky bright blue. The snowcapped mountains surrounded us. We went skiing at our favorite resort, Heavenly. Josh and I were on the chair lift in the middle of sheer heaven, and he was sharing his frustrations about work. At that moment I said to him, "If you can't unwind and enjoy this, then none of your work is worth it. It's just not worth the stress." This seemed to get through to him.

Even though he was earning more than he ever had before, we decided it wasn't worth his happiness. After weighing our options, we decided to start our own sales and marketing process consulting company. My mom said that she couldn't believe we would do this—walk away from a good, secure income into the complete unknown. Starting our own business was a big risk, but I had a good feeling about making this change. Josh did the front-end consulting, and I did the back-end business. He came up with the name of the company, Garrett Miller Associates. This warmed my heart. Even though he was able to negotiate a package out of his position, we didn't have a big cushion of money. We knew it would take time to ramp up a business from scratch, especially living three hours from the nearest major city. Finances were extremely tight for a while, but I always felt in the end we would do really well. It was stressful at times trying to figure out how to meet all our financial needs, and for months we watched every penny. It was a new way of living for us without a regular income—having money come in and making it last and not knowing when or from where more would come.

About six months into our marriage, I noticed that Josh seemed to drink heavily. Although he drank a six-pack almost every night, he neither seemed drunk, nor was he belligerent in any way. I was concerned, particularly for his health. When I brought up my concern, he was receptive. His response to me was, "Do you think I'm an alcoholic?" This surprised me, and I responded, "You are the only one who can answer that." I had dealt with Kevin's marijuana smoking, but he was not an alcoholic. I didn't know much about it, although there were members of my family (not my parents) who had issues with alcohol. I did tell him that I had already been with someone with an addiction, and I wasn't willing to have that experience again. I didn't insist he get help, and I didn't make any ultimatums. If he really wanted to make a change, it was going to have to come of his own desire. He was out of town when we had this conversation, so when he came home he began going to AA. He got a sponsor and seemed to work hard on making a change. Both Garrett and I fully supported him.

Within a relatively short time, we began earning more money than he had earned in his previous position. We continued to create a lifestyle beyond my dreams. We skied at Heavenly Ski Resort in the winter and spent the summers on our boat on the lake. Garrett loved to wakeboard. We had good friends in the community and hosted family holidays. We enjoyed all the offerings of Lake Tahoe. I had no intention of moving and thought I would live there the rest of my life. It was a happy time for our family.

My relationship with Josh was founded on friendship. We liked each other; we shared the same beliefs on spirituality, politics, and money. Sometimes we had different perspectives on parenting, but we could and did find common ground. Both Josh and I loved to travel. My favorite times were when we were together as a family, just having regular conversations. He and Garrett were witty, fun, and they made me laugh. We got along well in our day-to-day lives. My first marriage was difficult; this one was easy. Josh was generous and loving, and I adored him.

When we first married, neither of us had any intention of having more children. Josh had three daughters—eighteen, seventeen, and thirteen—and I had Garrett. Within our first year of marriage, things changed. I wanted to have a baby. We had a good thing going, and I wanted to share it. Josh did, too—so much, in fact, that he had a vasectomy reversal. It worked, but he had a low sperm count. We thought, Well, if it happens, great. In the meantime, we went on with life.

Garrett was an athlete. Growing up, he played soccer, baseball, basketball, and football. He was particularly interested in any sport that was on a board. He spent hours on his skateboard practicing. I would take him to the skate park or watch him practice in front of the house; there he would practice ollies, an impressive trick where Garrett and the board leap in the air without using his hands. He always wanted to show me a new trick. For quite a while, he pleaded a case for a half-pipe in the backyard or a picnic table to grind, which is sliding along an object on the skateboard trucks rather than using the wheels.

I first noticed we saw the world from a different perspective when he was a boy. He saw every stairway and handrail as something to ride or grind. While I saw these things as they appeared, he saw them as an adventure. He showed me how we could look at the same thing and have different perspectives. This awareness has helped me in many situations in my life.

We lived on top of a hill and didn't get many trick-or-treaters, so most kids would go to neighborhoods with flat streets. When Garrett was twelve, he had the bright idea to go trick-or-treating at our neighbors' houses the morning after Halloween with no costume. Later that day, Josh was talking to one of the neighbors, and he mentioned that Garrett had been trick-or-treating that morning and was glad to have gotten rid of all their leftover candy. Come to find out, Garrett had scored a ton of candy that morning from many neighbors who were happy to get rid of their leftover candy, and, of course, Garrett was happy to help them out. I was mortified on one hand but had to give him credit for his creativity on the other.

Garrett was always a bit ahead of his time. When TiVo came out, he'd said, "I can't believe it, Mom. I thought of that; I was going to invent that." I was surprised at his remark because I had no idea he was thinking about it. He was genuinely upset that he didn't invent it first. He was about twelve at the time.

He enjoyed Ranch dressing. I would buy it supersized at Costco because he used it on everything. When I saw him dipping his pizza in Ranch dressing, I was appalled. Now, they sell pizza and Ranch dip together, go figure. The same with music. He listened to underground music before many of these artists became popular.

In April of 2000, my grandfather passed at the age of eighty-four after a several-month illness with cancer. Since his passing, there have been many times when I have felt him with me. The first time was within a day or two of his passing. I was alone driving from Lake Tahoe to Reno, and I could feel his energy in the car. I knew that he was enjoying the beauty of the drive with me. I began talking to him in my head. It was the first time I'd engaged with someone in the nonphysical, and it was as normal as if he had been in his body in the seat next to me. It felt good to know that Grandpa was with me. It felt so natural that I really didn't think much of it.

At the same time I was connecting with my grandfather, I began to notice, particularly with people who are close to me, that I could sense what they were thinking. I could feel when others were thinking of me when we were physically separated. I could also sense when someone was going to call and even sense when someone I knew was receiving a call. These connections began happening more frequently.

A couple of years after Josh and I married, we moved into a new house located in Zephyr Cove on the Nevada side of the lake. We loved this house, too. It had more room, better office space, and beautiful lake views. This meant we would be in a different school district. I offered to arrange for Garrett to stay in the same junior high school, but he decided to change schools. He was in the eighth grade.

At this time, even though I was aware of my intuitive knowing, I was not completely present to it. I never considered myself a psychic. I had consulted with psychics a few different times and was told that I was psychic, but I never took it seriously. There was a part of me that didn't want to own it. I believed that I wasn't, although I was naturally operating in an intuitive way. I didn't know it was as easy as it was. I didn't realize that being psychic or intuitive was the same.

Family vacations are an important part of my life. From the time Garrett was five, I'd made family vacations a priority. I've always felt that having experiences together makes life more meaningful. To me vacations are like adventures, and Garrett was always up for an adventure. Fortunately, when I married Josh, he enjoyed travel, too. As a family we agreed to allow fun in our lives often.

It was never easy leaving our paradise in Lake Tahoe, but we did enjoy other adventures. The three of us traveled all over the world. We went to Disney World and Disneyland more times than I can count.

On our first anniversary, Josh took me to Italy. We stayed for almost three weeks, traveling to Rome, Florence, and Venice. All of Josh's business travel paid off in that we were able to fly first class. The entire vacation was first class. This was by far the most breathtaking and romantic trip we took. It was also the longest vacation I had ever taken. It was my first trip to Europe and the longest I had been away from Garrett. My parents stayed in Tahoe and took care of Garrett, our dogs and cats.

For my fortieth birthday, Josh took me to Paris to celebrate. We wanted Garrett to experience this with us. He loved Paris; we all did.

When we traveled, Garrett always wanted to sit up front, next to the cab drivers, to ask them questions about their life or the city we were in; he was always naturally curious. During our marriage, we made several trips to Hawaii. One trip was to celebrate Josh's fortieth birthday. On this trip, he and Garrett swam with dolphins. Garrett learned to surf while in Hawaii and spent quite a bit of time riding waves. It seemed to come easily to him. He's reminding me of how much we both loved the fresh virgin pineapple margaritas in Hawaii.

CHAPTER SIX

Manhattan, September 2001

With ordinary consciousness you can't
even begin to know what's happening.
—Saul Bell, The Dean's December

In 2001, my mother and I went to Manhattan to celebrate her sixty-fifth birthday, which was on September 10. Before our leaving, I had some reservations about the trip but was not willing to cancel it and disappoint her. She had always wanted to go to New York. It was dark and rainy the afternoon of the tenth when we moved from our hotel in midtown to a fairly new hotel, the Embassy Suites, downtown. We planned for a morning shopping spree at a designer discount store located in the Twin Towers.

On the morning of September 11, my mother was putting on her makeup while I was in the shower. When I got out, she asked me, "Did you hear that noise?" I said, "No, I didn't hear anything." We had the TV on and shortly afterward saw on TV a plane fly into one of the towers. We wondered if we could see it from our hotel. It had been dark and raining when we checked in, and we didn't know exactly where we were in proximity. Looking out our bedroom window, we couldn't believe our eyes. We could clearly see the burning tower. It felt as if we could reach out and touch the tower because it was so close. Not long after, the hotel manager came over a loudspeaker system throughout the hotel and told everyone to stay put. From our window we saw crowds gathering below. There were ambulances lining up on the street, and people were setting up tables—to help injured people right on the street. Looking back, I think we were all in a state of shock. Here was this major disaster: the tower burning, people watching, some getting their children out of school. They, too, were watching from the sidewalk. Fear hadn't set in. The onlookers were watching the scene as if it were a casual event.

I called home and Garrett answered. I talked to him for a moment and then asked him to get Josh. They were on West Coast time, so it was still quite early for them. I explained what was happening, and Josh began watching the events on CNN.

Events continued to unfold, and the Pentagon and second tower were hit. Shortly after the second tower was hit, we heard and felt the first tower collapse. It felt like an earthquake. The room shook, and all the lights in the room were flickering. Then we heard an announcement over the loudspeaker to evacuate the building immediately, to use emergency exits, not the elevator. Now this was serious. First we were told to stay put, and now it was time to hightail it out of the hotel. We called home, letting our family know we were being evacuated. We took our purses—that was it. We left our luggage behind, not thinking we wouldn't be able to return to our room.

Even though it was chaotic, it was quiet. Cellular service was on overload and only available for emergency responders. The F-15's flying overhead were ominous, a sign that we were in a war zone. It was eerie. We had no communication; we did not know what was happening or what would happen. I remember thinking, *This is what it's like in countries that have wars.* It was a surreal experience. I felt as if we were in a movie, and we would soon see Bruce Willis or Arnold Schwarzenegger come blazing down the street. People were walking in complete silence, in a state of shock. It was incomprehensible the magnitude of what was happening. There were no cars on the road, no yellow taxis, no traffic. And worse, we rarely heard an ambulance siren. No one was going to the hospitals. There were hundreds walking in shock and disbelief, many covered in ashes. The ash, I had noticed, looked exactly the same as the ash from Mt. St. Helens, when it erupted in 1980. In the moment it seemed strange that office equipment, steel, and human bodies would be the same substance as volcanic ash.

After the evacuation, my mother and I had no idea where we were—no map, no guidebook. We just fell in line and began walking with the crowd. We stopped for a moment and stood to the side of the crowd and looked back at the last burning tower. As we watched the flames and people emptying from buildings, the second tower fell. It was as if a bomb went off. The only thing I could see was a plume of black smoke and people running for their lives. We were far enough away that we did not get caught up in the smoke, but we did turn and continued to follow the rest of the crowd walking away from what is now known as Ground Zero.

We stopped at a local bar that was open and watched CNN's reporting of the events. We sat for a while trying to comprehend what was happening and discussing where we were going to go. The bar was packed with many people covered in ash telling their stories. It was clear we would not be able to go back to our hotel. We had reservations at the Waldorf for the following evening, and we were hoping we might be able to check in early. Since Manhattan was evidently on lockdown, hotel opportunities were diminishing. We were worried we wouldn't have a place to stay. After many attempts, I was able to get through to my husband from a landline pay phone at the bar. He had seen the towers fall while watching the events unfold on CNN and knew there was no way we would be able to return to our room. So, he immediately began making calls to get us a room.

Josh told me that if we could get to the Waldorf, they would have a room for us. This was a huge relief, but where was the Waldorf? We had no idea—no idea where we were, for that matter. We asked for directions and began walking again.

It was still ominously quiet on the streets. There was a digital sign that said the stock market was closed. We walked past Madison Square Garden. There was a huge billboard promoting Oregon Duck quarterback, Joey Harrington, for the Heisman trophy. It was as if we were on an empty movie lot—familiar places and expected scenery but chillingly silent. We kept walking.

We eventually found the Waldorf, and the staff was wonderful. Our room was waiting for us; it was a relief to finally have a place to be and to assimilate what had happened. Over the next several days, while at the Waldorf Astoria, there were constant alerts of bomb threats at the hotel and throughout the city. People entering the hotel were subject to having their bags and purses searched, but no one seemed to mind this new procedure. Everyone seemed patient and courteous. There was compassion in the air. The city had a completely different vibe than it did a few days before.

On the streets there were evening vigils and pictures posted everywhere of missing loved ones. At first there were many requests for blood donations because of concern there would be a shortage, and the emergency rooms would be full by the end of the day. But this was not the case. The most haunting part for me at the time, after both towers had come down, was the silence. That there were no ambulance sirens was heartbreaking we all knew this probably meant very few survived the towers' collapse. It was impossible not to feel the tremendous pain of the city. We were stranded in Manhattan for several days as the entire island was on lockdown. It was also several days before flights were opened up again at LaGuardia, which was the last airport in the country to reopen.

After returning home I experienced post-traumatic stress disorder. My heart would begin racing for no particular reason, often waking me up in the middle of the night. I would also have difficulty falling back to sleep. I couldn't watch anything with any kind of violence on TV. I remember my husband watching the miniseries *Band of Brothers*. I couldn't stay in the room; it was too much. This went on for a year.

CHAPTER SEVEN

Back in Portland

You have to accept whatever comes, and the
only important thing is that you meet it with courage
and with the best that you have to give.
—Eleanor Roosevelt

Although Kevin often promised Garrett he would come to visit him in Tahoe in the six years we lived there, he never came. Even though I knew Kevin was not in a good way, he was Garrett's father, and Garrett loved him. For Garrett I wanted him to have a relationship with his father. Josh and I supported Garrett's visits to Portland to see Kevin, and he had regular phone contact with Kevin.

Since Garrett was twelve, he attended Windells Snowboard Camp on Mt. Hood in Oregon, forty-five minutes east of Portland. The summer of 2001, he planned to stay in Portland with Kevin for a week following camp.

Toward the end of the eighth grade, Garrett started getting in trouble at school. When he came home from this trip in Portland, his level of mischief escalated. At first I didn't know what was prompting his behavior. I was frustrated because it didn't make any sense to me.

Soon it became quite clear. In the fall, we discovered Garrett had taken my new 4Runner out joyriding and caused some damage to it. This was a serious event and prompted Josh to call and apprise Kevin. The result was a fallout between Kevin, Garrett, and me that lasted over four years.

It turned out that Kevin had been encouraging Garrett to get in trouble. He had told him that if he got into enough trouble, I would eventually let Garrett come live with him. So, of course, the boy who wanted nothing more than his father's approval and acceptance was doing everything he could to please his father. Garrett confessed to me that while he had been visiting Kevin over the summer, Kevin was smoking pot and encouraged Garrett to smoke it with him, which he did. It was a revelation I could scarcely fathom. If encouraging his son to get in trouble and to get him started on drugs wasn't appalling enough, Kevin offered *to take Garrett off our hands* if he could quit paying the court-ordered child support. In the end, Garrett was used and manipulated by Kevin as a pawn in trying to get out of paying child support. It was sickening. Kevin denied he instigated the bad behavior from Garrett, who was devastated at being betrayed by his father. After this information was revealed, I called Kevin on the phone and had a heated conversation with him. I threatened to turn him in to authorities for his behavior in getting his fourteen-year-old son to smoke pot, and I let him know I wasn't going to be sending Garrett for anymore visits. Any loving parent can imagine the resolve and force I spoke to Kevin with. I left nothing uncertain—or unsaid—in protecting my son. Kevin didn't push back.

I had always tried to protect Garrett from his father and make excuses for his behavior, but this time I didn't. I explained to Garrett that Kevin wasn't in his right mind and that someone who had been smoking pot all those years, encouraging him to get in trouble, and getting him started on drugs could not possibly be thinking clearly. My words didn't ease his pain. A few days later, Garrett told me he sent Kevin an e-mail and asked him, "What kind of man encourages his son to get in trouble? What kind of man gets his son to do drugs?" He signed the e-mail "Garrett Miller." After this incident, Kevin never tried to contact Garrett. It wasn't until Garrett was eighteen that Garrett reached out to Kevin.

I thought it would be helpful if Garrett went to a counselor to help him better understand that his father's behavior had nothing to do with him.

Still smarting from the trauma of September 11, I began longing to be closer to my childhood friends and my family. Josh had already mentioned he would like to live in Portland. I was also feeling that a change, closer to family, might also be good for Garrett. The culmination of emotions I was feeling triggered a move back to Portland. I was not in the best state of mind to make a huge decision, but I did. Within a year of September 11, I literally ran home. We moved back to Portland, something I never dreamed I would do.

We moved back to West Linn, where Garrett and I lived before we moved to Tahoe. We rented a house while we searched for a home in the area to buy. During the summer of 2002, I began reading a book called *Sacred Contracts* by Caroline Myss. It offered some ideas about spirituality that I had not considered before. The premise of the book is that we all are born with pre-birth contracts to fulfill during our lifetime. For example, we have agreements to meet certain people, and we have archetypes that reflect our personalities and interests. Some of us might be artists, scientists, teachers, and so on, but we use our free will to decide how to fulfill our contract. I was familiar with archetypes from some of the Jungian courses I took while in college. This book, though, inspired me to reflect. What contracts could I identify? Certainly having my son was a contract; there was nothing random in his being born. So were my relationships, my marriages. The idea of pre-birth agreements resonated with me. Another piece of the puzzle was put into place.

The book helped me to again see life from a new perspective, one that was not random but planned out by me before I was born or incarnated into my body. It was a key piece of information that has helped me many times throughout my life. I began to understand there was a purpose to things that happened in my life, even if I didn't understand the purpose in the moment. I was beginning to learn that nothing is random.

When Garrett was growing up, he was interested in Josh's marine field training, particularly survival skills, land navigation, and the improvise, adapt, and overcome model, which is training in dealing with challenges and obstacles. Garrett was still reacting to and having difficulty recovering from the issues with Kevin.He had been getting into a fair amount of trouble was emotionally hurt.

Josh thought Garrett would greatly benefit from a wilderness challenge. He felt it would raise Garrett's self-esteem and provide him with a new level of self-confidence and sense of accomplishment. There was also a spiritual component to the program.

Having heard Outward Bound had a good program, Josh signed them up for a father–son leadership expedition. It was an intense, week-long expedition in the North Cascades National Forest which is part of the Cascade Mountain Range in Washington State. The trip included hiking, rock climbing, rappelling down mountains, and cross-county land navigation.

They went on the expedition in 2002, the summer we returned to the Portland area. Garrett was fifteen. During the trip, Garrett's compassion, leadership, and sense of humor shined. Josh said he thrived. He was comfortable and able to be all of who he was in this environment.

Garrett felt connected; he belonged in the outdoors. There was plenty of discomfort from the physical endurance. The mosquitos were so intense in some places that they wore mosquito masks. During the trip he never complained about anything; nothing got him down.

There was a smaller teenager in the group who, after a few days, was having difficulty with his heavy pack. Garrett had the boy take several items out of his pack, which lightened it considerably, put them in his own, and carried them for the boy. Each day the guide gave the group a choice of going either a longer, easier route or a shorter route with difficult terrain. Garrett chose the shorter, more difficult terrain and was often outvoted.

When they returned from the trip, both Josh and Garrett were beaming and excited to share the experience. I could see something positive in Garrett: his level of self-confidence, his growth. Josh was right about the trip. I could also see they had a deeper connection.

I loved hearing the stories they shared. In all the stories he shared with me, Garrett never mentioned helping the boy. That came from Josh. Garrett didn't think twice about it.

Josh told me the trip was the most worthwhile investment he had ever made.

After months of searching, we found our dream home in the Stafford area, not far from the condo Garrett and I lived in when I was going to school. It was a fairy-tale setting on two acres. A beautiful fountain with white roses surrounding it created an enchanting welcoming to the house. Beautiful mature cherry, willow, and fir trees and large hydrangea bushes, pink roses, and boxwoods adorned the landscape. There was a secret garden located off the great room that was surrounded by arborvitae, and a pergola was covered in pink roses and jasmine, a sweet-smelling canopy. The master suite had a fireplace, a deck, and his and her bathrooms. We also had office spaces. My dream kitchen had commercial appliances and a beautiful view from the large kitchen window. The great room was massive with a huge stone fireplace and large floor-to-ceiling windows that brought the old-growth trees and blue hydrangeas into the landscape of the room. Downstairs was the family room, two more bedrooms with a Jack and Jill bath, and the laundry room. The doors of both downstairs bedrooms opened up to a patio with spectacular views. The five-car garage was attached to a guesthouse and storage galore. It even had the trampoline Garrett had always wanted. Even though the downstairs needed remodeling, this home had everything each of us wanted. It was evident to me, each time I moved, the next house was my next dream home. As we first walked the grounds, I clearly remember thinking that Garrett could get married here, and this would be the home we would live in forever.

Not long after we returned to Portland, I became pregnant. We were all overjoyed with the news and filled with anticipation for the baby. I was pregnant when we were remodeling the downstairs of our house. It was a big project, and I became anemic and was extremely fatigued during my pregnancy. During this time, I was less involved with the business as I was focusing on the remodeling and my pregnancy.

Garrett was sixteen when Ryan was born. My doctor who delivered Garrett also delivered Ryan. When I had a cesarean section, Garrett was in the surgery room with Josh and me. He was concerned and a little scared for me; I could see it on his face. I was nauseated from the pain medication and couldn't stop shaking, but he sat with me and held my hand. He was so caring and loving with me and with his new baby brother.

Born with a full head of dark hair, Ryan came into this world tipping the scale at ten pounds. When I was pregnant with him, I could barely breathe. Toward the end of the pregnancy, I could feel him wiggling all the time; the poor little guy just didn't have any room. I remember saying, "This baby is different," and he was compared to Garrett, who was an average-sized baby and weighed seven pounds and five ounces when he was born.

Garrett adored Ryan and enjoyed being an older brother. (It's hard for me to write in the past tense here because it's still true.) Garrett was always sweet and tender with Ryan.

Garrett and I have always been close. We had our ups and downs. We brought out the best and, at times, the worst, in each other. We didn't always listen to one another, but we tried. He always had his own mind and would not be controlled (I was recently reminded that he was like his mother in this regard), which, at times, drove me crazy. Gaining his cooperation rather than trying to break his spirit was a challenge for me. When he was six, I took him to a psychologist, and he told me Garrett was a strong-willed child. The psychologist further explained this meant he would be a challenge to raise; however, he would make a great CEO when he grew up.

For many years I read books on spirituality. I couldn't get enough. Every time I had another question, I would find a new book with the answer. Although I didn't realize it, I was preparing for what was to happen when Garrett transitioned. My intense spiritual journey had begun.

When Garrett was a teenager, there were times I had little influence over him. There were many times when he pushed the envelope, and I felt he was out of control. Garrett gave me many opportunities to apply what I was learning, but I was rarely appreciative of the opportunities I was being given. After Kevin's heinous intentions were revealed, Garrett never seemed to fully recover. He continued smoking pot, and eventually this took a toll on his and our lives. We did everything we could to help Garrett get the tools he needed. Nothing seemed to work for long.

I thought parents were here to teach their children. This is true in some respects: they teach accountability, the importance of an academic education, what it means to be true to themselves, and the basics of getting along in the world. What I have come to realize is our children are here to teach us. When our children push our buttons, they aren't doing it to torture us; rather, they are helping us learn more about ourselves. It's not about them; it's about us. Garrett was doing what he agreed to do: to help teach me to trust myself, let go of judgment, become tolerant, and to know unconditional love. I had heard many times before that those around us are a mirror, so that we can see ourselves. If we don't like what we see, we can change our way of being, and that will also reflect itself back.

Clearly, I was doing something wrong. I didn't have the right parenting tools. It was time to try something new. We sent him to a local rehab for teens, but he hated it and didn't do well there.

Since he'd had a good experience with Outward Bound, we sent him to an outdoor camp for kids, hoping this would help. He didn't want to go, but when he came back, he was happy and appreciative of the experience. He learned a lot about himself and loved being in nature, learning wilderness techniques.

When Garrett returned from wilderness camp, he was excited to share with me a book he had read during what was called "solo." Solo was three days of no contact with anyone else. He had built his own camp in the snow and had his journal and the book he was given to read. The book was called *The Alchemist* by Paulo Coelho. Garrett loved the book and couldn't wait to share it with me. I didn't read it until about a year later, and when I read it I understood why he loved it so much. It's about a boy on a journey, learning to trust his guidance and the signs along the way. It's a beautiful story of alchemy.

I believe when Garrett was in nature, he was happy and at peace. It was as if he could always find himself in this environment. When he returned from this experience, he was the boy I always knew he was. Seeing his light again made my heart sing.

Things were back on track for a while. He was having fun at school; he had a girlfriend who was a good influence; and overall things were going well.

When Garrett was six, I bought a Mustang Convertible. My mother wasn't thrilled with the idea of me driving a Mustang. I understood her perspective, but this was a different kind of car—an automatic, four cylinder, not the fast model my father was driving at the time of his passing. I'd had the car for quite a while, and Garrett had wanted us to keep it for him when he was ready to drive. I thought it was a good car for Garrett to drive after he got his driver's license. He wouldn't be able to get much speed in that car, but he was happy to have a car to drive.

Garrett was excited to start driving. He tested for his driver's license when he turned sixteen. Shortly after Garrett got his license, Josh was driving home and saw that Garrett's Mustang was parked on the side of the road, not far from our house. The hood of the car was up, and Garrett was looking underneath trying to solve some problem. Later we discovered he had blown out the transmission because he had been driving the car like a manual transmission rather than an automatic.

Garrett's love of nature inspired him to find special spots that had spectacular views. He seemed to have a knack for finding them. Eager to share the special treat, he would take me to some treasure he'd found in nature. Watching a sunset with him was the best. These were some of the most precious times we shared.

Garrett enjoyed all kinds of music, particularly rap. While music playing in his room when he was a teenager was expected, the genre of music could be a surprise. I tried to censor some of it, but it was a battle I couldn't win. Even though I didn't like the messages in some of the rap music he listened to, he enjoyed sharing with me the occasional song that he liked. He seemed to enjoy the challenge of finding and sharing a song that he liked, onc that I would like, too. Bob Marley's *Three Little Birds* is our family theme song. We love it.

Garrett always kissed and hugged me good-bye. It didn't matter if his friends were around or not. There was nothing better than a hug from Garrett. Whenever we talked on the phone, he would tell me he loved me. Garrett enjoyed movies. His favorites were *The Shawshank Redemption* and *Rudy*.

Garrett continued to do more than his fair share of shenanigans. During his high school years, a call from the school counselor was a regular event. It scared me. We couldn't seem to communicate at that time, and I feared I was losing him. Nothing gave me more joy than when Garrett would smile. It was contagious and could light up a room Nothing scared me more than when his light was not shining, when I felt I couldn't reach him.

For whatever reason, I don't remember why, but being rebellious, Garrett ran away from home when he was sixteen, taking the car with him. He drove to Lake Tahoe. Once we figured out where he was, I was on the next plane to bring him home.

At the airport waiting to board my flight, I felt frustrated with my son and myself, wondering how we could get things on track. It was obvious I had no control over him. Besides, trying to control him never worked. I was desperate to know how I could influence him in a positive way. I decided to go to the bookstore to see if I could find a book that would help me in this situation. I prayed to be led to the perfect book, and I was not disappointed. It was the only book that spoke to me, and really it was easy to notice considering the title: *There's a Spiritual Solution to Every Problem* by Wayne Dyer. Thank you, God, for answering my prayer!

I began reading while waiting at the gate and hated to put it down when the plane landed. I could physically feel relief in my heart when I read this book. My anxiety had begun to lift shortly after I began this book. I could feel the anger and frustration leave my body, and I felt love and compassion for Garrett. I felt myself transforming. The teachings and the tools in Dr. Dyer's book were exactly what I had hoped to find. I knew, no matter what was going on in the moment, all was going to be OK.

There were many parts of the book that spoke to me, all of them highlighted on the many dog-eared pages. One that struck me and has stayed with me is a quote from the book *A Course in Miracles*: "I can choose peace, rather than this." Remembering this buoyed me during that time, and many times since in my most challenging moments. I had tools I could use to help me, and by using them things began to change for the better.

After a few days, I still hadn't found Garrett. I flew back home because I didn't want to be away from Ryan while he was still a baby. Within a few days, I returned to Tahoe. This time I drove the eleven hours and was determined to find him. It was Mother's Day weekend, and I found him staying at a friend's house. He was ready to come home. I wasn't mad at him, and he was sorry to have put us through the stress. He drove the Mustang, and I followed him home in the car I drove. We stayed the night in Ashland, Oregon. I felt our connection again. We talked about what happened and why. And, of course, we agreed not to do this one again. There was no arguing or blaming, just an openness and connection. My boy was back.

Around that time, Josh was interested in Kabbalah, which is Jewish mysticism. I began to study it with him. I read many books on Kabbalah, the teachings of which deeply resonated with me. One of the books I read was on reincarnation. While it was completely foreign to the beliefs of my upbringing in the Christian church, it made complete sense and confirmed other sources I'd read that had touched upon the idea of reincarnation. It was at this time that I became unafraid of the idea of death. It wasn't a major revelation but a gradual awakening of my knowing. I was no longer the frightened little girl lying in bed late at night in fear of dying.

Kabbalists are big fans of meditation, and I began meditating several times a day. This practice showed results fairly quickly in my way of being, and I noticed I was more relaxed. Some things began to fall in place easier than they had in the past. I had a book of meditations, and if I became stressed or worried about something, I would look for a meditation to help me focus on what I wanted. As I continued meditating, things in my life began to shift. Internally, I felt more peaceful and loving. I was sharing my learning and thoughts about it with Garrett, and though he was open to it, he wasn't always in the mood. It had to be when he was wanting the connection—not when I thought he should want it.

Chapter Eight

Chaos or Divine Order

Should you shield the canyon from the windstorms you would never see the beauty of their carvings.
—Elisabeth Kubler-Ross

I know he tried, but as most people do, Garrett slipped back with old friends followed by old habits. At the time, I didn't know that treatment centers have a low rate of success. I felt I was on the verge of losing Garrett, and I didn't know what to do. He was still underage and my responsibility. I had a firm conviction that while he was still under my watch, I was going to do everything I could to help him. It came down to sending him away to a treatment facility where he was able to get clean and finish his education. Prior to that, we'd sent him to another outdoor program for teens. It was a huge struggle. He didn't want to go, but at this point he had no alternative; he was going.

After he resigned to going, he was a model student. He loved being in the wilderness and learning new things. He also made good friends. I went to pick him up from the program, and the kids had a special ceremony that showcased the skills they had learned while in the wilderness. It was quite impressive. We were standing in a big circle—the parents, teens, and counselors. Each kid would go in the middle of the circle and show a skill and share something he or she had learned. There was one boy who was trying to start fire with flint. He kept trying, but it wasn't happening, and the more he tried, the more nervous he was. All eyes were on him, and every time he tried, nothing. I could feel the boy's stress and nerves and felt compassion for him. This went on for several minutes. Given the circumstances, it felt like a long time. For him it must have felt like an eternity. And he seemed to get increasingly flustered. Without being asked, Garrett stepped into the middle with the boy, got on his knees next to him, and began talking the boy through it very calmly. The boy relaxed, and Garrett encouraged him and stepped him through it until the boy got the fire started. This was and is one of my proudest moments of Garrett. His compassion, his steadfastness for his peer, and his patience and encouragement for this boy overwhelmed me. Later when we were driving home, I asked Garrett about the boy. He told me it was the one kid that he didn't really connect with, which made it more remarkable to me that he supported this boy in the way that he did. Garrett downplayed his actions by saying he was hungry and knew when the boy finished we would get to eat. That was Garrett.

Garrett was invited back to the wilderness program as a mentor. He was excited to have this opportunity. After he finished school he went back and completed an internship at the wilderness program. He loved helping the other kids and later was offered a job. He decided not to take it because he did not want to move across the country. There were other things that he wanted to try.

After Ryan was born, I noticed that Josh seemed to be struggling. Sometimes he would overreact to situations. Although Garrett gave him plenty of opportunities to get angry, Josh would go over the top at times over what seemed to me small things that didn't have anything to do with Garrett. We all get angry, but when Josh got angry, he would also become verbally abusive. He did this on a number of occasions with Garrett. This sometimes happened in counseling sessions Josh would get over the top angry, and the counselors didn't acknowledge it, like it was OK. The counselors would look the other way. I would wait for them to just acknowledge his behavior, but no one ever really called him on it. I looked away for a while, too, but there came a point when I told him it was something he needed to deal with, that I wasn't willing to live with his anger. It was clear the velocity of his anger was not about someone else but about something within that had strong energy behind it.

I also noticed Josh having mood swings. At the time I chalked it up to stress of the remodeling, his frustrations with parenting, and his contemplating a career change. I was consumed with being a better person, mother, and wife. Garrett was working hard as well on making positive choices. Little Ryan was a sweet, happy baby, but my husband seemed to be falling apart. It didn't make any sense to me. I was taking what I thought were the steps toward a happy marriage and family. How could this be happening? He was my rock. During my meditations, I would try to visualize us all together in our home, and I couldn't see it.

Since my first clear vision of living in Lake Tahoe, I began to notice how often I had such visions. I get a vision of something; it might be how I want my house to be or a place I want to go, and eventually it would come to fruition. Also, there were times when I tried to create a vision about something, but I couldn't see it. A couple of times I tried to envision my family a certain way and it just wouldn't happen. Now, I realize when I can't see it, it means it's not going to happen my way. I'll get the essence of it but not exactly how I tried to picture it.

I was building a vision of the life I wanted, and I could easily picture Garrett and me working together, but when I tried to envision him in a place, I couldn't see him there. I tried. I could see other people but not Garrett. Now I understand why. It's best that I didn't know why at the time. I interpreted that he would be living somewhere else, which was accurate, but I never thought he'd be living in nonphysical.

During our marriage, I always felt close to Josh. I could talk to him about anything. I thought we were on the same page spiritually. I thought we had the same values. After all, we loved our family, and I trusted him with my life. We had dreams we had accomplished together, and we had more to fulfill.

Our marriage began to unravel a few months after Garrett left for school. I went to visit Garrett, and Josh stayed home with Ryan. When I came home, there was a different energy in the air. He was distant—even though when I had arrived in my hotel room, he had a dozen red roses waiting for me. When I came home, something felt different, but I couldn't place it.

A couple of weeks after I returned, Josh and I had an intense conversation. He told me he had turned in all his AA anniversary chips. I asked him why, and he said he wasn't doing his work and was behaving like a dry drunk. Then, all of his recent behavior made sense to me. I supported him in his choicc to continue his AA program.

Shortly after, we took a family trip to spend Thanksgiving with Garrett and spend time in Tahoe. I told Garrett about Josh's turning in his AA anniversary chips, and he thought that it was a strange thing to do. Still, we had a special time with Garrett over the Thanksgiving holiday. My heart was singing. He looked great; he was happy; and he was doing well. Little Ryan was toddling around, and they would play. Garrett taught him basketball. It was a good visit, and we all had a good time together.

It felt good to be back in Tahoe. I was soaking up the energy and the beautiful scenery. There was about a foot and a half of snow covering the ground, and the holiday decorations adorned the town. I always missed living in Tahoe and wanted to get a second home there at some point. We spent an afternoon driving around, looking at houses. One evening we went to our friend's house for dinner. They had bought a house before we moved and completely remodeled it. It was fun to see the stunning home they created. At some point during the evening, though, Josh overreacted over something we were talking about; it might have been about getting a second home. I can't remember what prompted his fierce reaction. I do remember it seemed to come from left field, and it was uncomfortable for everyone. His intensity died down, and the rest of the evening went fine. When we returned to our hotel, we discussed it. We didn't argue—just discussed it, and he apologized.

On New Year's Eve day, we had a conference call with Garrett's counselor. Although the call went well, Josh seemed distant. When I asked him if anything was bothering him, he said he was fine and was going to an AA meeting and then to the grocery store. I had scheduled a massage late that afternoon with a gift certificate Josh had given me for Christmas. Our friends had invited us out, but we decided to stay home with Ryan and make a special dinner.

When he returned from the store, I left for my massage. I called him when I was in the car driving home to let him know I would be home soon and to check on Ryan who was napping. When I pulled up to the front of the house, I had a foreshadowing. The song *Landslide* by Stevie Nicks was playing on the radio. I sat there for a moment listening to the song before I went inside. I was looking forward to spending the evening with Josh and Ryan.

I was in no way prepared for what was to happen, which, for some strange reason, was the plan. As I walked in, Josh was at the door, profusely sweating and getting ready to leave. I asked him what was going on, but he wouldn't answer me. Then I asked him where he was going, and he still wouldn't answer me. All he said was, "You'll know on Monday." I said, "You can't leave like this." But he could, and he did.

I was shattered. As I came into the house, I could see he had moved some furniture out, and Ryan was just waking up from his nap. The anguish, confusion, and betrayal I felt shook me to my core. I was at an all-time low and completely and intentionally blindsided. It was a calculated act of cruelty directed at me, who adored him. Being New Year's Eve, all my friends were out for the evening. I had no friend to call for support or to help me with Ryan. I didn't want to upset my family until I understood what was happening.

My mind was spinning, but I had to find some strength within me to take care of Ryan without completely falling apart. Somehow I did; it was the longest weekend of my life. When I shared what happened with a couple of my closest friends, they too were shocked.

The following Monday, I was served divorce papers and discovered Josh had cleared out all our bank accounts. I had no money. To say I was surprised was putting it mildly. We rarely argued. We never threatened divorce or talked about it in any way. I realized he was drinking, something he knew I wouldn't allow in my life. That was the only thing that could explain this behavior.

Over the next month and a half, we talked, and I finally persuaded him to come home and get help. What Josh shared was sad, and now the relinquishing of his AA chips made sense. He told me that he had been drinking during our entire marriage, and that's why he turned in his chips. He had only ever been three months' sober. I was shocked, although I could see how easy it would be for him to drink since he traveled a fair amount. And that's just what he did. He had been living a lie for almost seven years.

Josh told me it was difficult for him to see Garrett doing so well, while he was not. He went back to AA, got a sponsor, and began his process of sobriety. He seemed to be trying. We decided not to tell Garrett. We didn't want him to worry about us and I didn't want anything to get in the way of Garrett's sobriety program.

Garrett came home a month later. He was happy, doing well, and he had gotten a job. Josh seemed to be back on track, more like his true self. Mother's Day 2005 started off perfect. Our little family went to brunch. It felt good to be together. We were laughing and having a wonderful day. Later in the early evening, I had a strange conversation with Josh. He was distant again. When I asked him about it, he blew me off. The next morning, he had left early for an AA meeting and came home with a bouquet of flowers for me. Something was off. I could feel it.

In the early afternoon, I left with Ryan to run errands with the understanding Josh was going to pick up Garrett from work. Ryan and I came home, but Garrett and Josh were not home yet. Shortly after I arrived home, Garrett called and said that Josh was two hours late picking him up. Josh was never late. He was always Johnny on the spot. Something was really wrong. Rather than being worried, I was angry. Shortly after that call, Josh brought Garrett home. I asked where he had been, and he defensively asked me the same thing. An argument ensued, and he took some clothes and left. That was it. I knew it was over.

I was heartbroken, even though I knew it was the best solution for all concerned. My heart and head were in a good place, and I had taken myself to a new level. I couldn't believe Josh wasn't going to come with me. It was difficult to believe he would choose alcohol over this family. We had a beautiful life. I was disappointed. I thought we were spiritual partners. It took me awhile, but eventually I had to accept it. We were moving in opposite directions. Since then I discovered the Law of Attraction and learned when the vibrational distance gets too great, you can't have others of a lower vibration in your space—like attracts like, birds of a feather, and all of that. Understanding this helped me as I was logically and emotionally sorting out my life. What was mine? What wasn't? How do I want to be going forward? I was processing all of it.

Josh, for some unknown reason, turned on Garrett during the divorce, which angered me and hurt Garrett. Here was another father figure turning his back on him. It was during this time, Father's Day 2005, I suggested to Garrett he reach out to Kevin. He hesitated but he did, and they began to revive their relationship. I soon regretted my suggestion when I saw that Kevin was blaming Garrett for the lapse in their relationship, taking no responsibility for his part. He was who he was, and it was clear he had no intention of changing. And Garrett accepted him, and in kind I supported Garrett.

This experience was completely different from my divorce with Garrett's father. I didn't feel the guilt for Ryan like I had for Garrett. I was disappointed, but Ryan was so young that somehow I knew he'd be OK. I felt bad that Garrett had to experience divorce again, as he was also heartbroken.

The divorce became vicious, which I didn't expect. I felt attacked and victimized. I tried to stay centered and grounded. For the most part, I did well, but I had my moments where I felt and responded otherwise. I was good at holding my thoughts to myself, but inside I was hurt and holding anger. Much later I learned about empaths, someone who picks up the energy and thoughts of others. I realized that I am an empath and was picking up and carrying Josh's anger, too. It wasn't always my own. It was a miserable experience.

My world was crashing down around me, and I was questioning my judgment, second-guessing the past. Was everything Josh ever told me a lie? Did I not fully appreciate all that I had? Why was it being taken away? Those and similar questions went through my mind like the running script on CNN. It was as if someone had killed my husband, and I didn't recognize this other person. It was bizarre. There was comfort for me in that our friends and my family couldn't believe it either. They were surprised at his behavior as well. I heard comments like, "I always thought he was such a stand-up guy."

Much of the pain came from the realization that, in essence, I had married the same man twice. It was staring me in the face. Although the outward packaging and the marriages were completely different, they both had a similar challenge, and there was no denying the common denominator was me.

I began getting visions. My dreams were giving me information and answering questions. All the meditation I had done helped me tap into my intuition.

I strongly felt my dad who had passed all those years ago. For the first time I could remember, I knew he was with me. One evening I was sitting in a chair in my bedroom crying, asking God for help, and I could feel my dad near me. He was unmistakable, even though he transitioned many years before. I recognized his energy and knew without a doubt he was with me. It was comforting yet mind-blowing. My tears over the breakup of my marriage became tears of love, joy, and appreciation for my connection with my father. Knowing he was with me at this moment reassured me I was not alone; he was there supporting me. He was there when I needed him, even though I couldn't see him. It makes me teary eyed remembering as I write this; it was so beautiful.

In the summer of 2005, a dear friend of Garrett's—Kyle—passed of an overdose. Everyone was stunned. Garrett took it hard; he adored Kyle. Kyle was a talented artist and athlete. When he came to our house, he always took time to play with Ryan. Kyle had a charming innocence about him. After Kyle's passing, Garrett got a tattoo on his upper right arm in honor of Kyle. It said "R.I.P. KB [that's what Garrett called him—KB] AKA KAOS 1." When I asked him what KAOS 1 meant, he said, "Peace." It was Kyle's signature on his art.

Garrett was heartbroken over Kyle's passing. He had a T-shirt made to wear to Kyle's funeral. Garrett wanted to pay tribute to Kyle; he truly loved him. Kyle's funeral was well attended by Kyle's family and friends. Kyle's body was there in an open casket. When Garrett saw Kyle's body, he collapsed. When Kyle's father spoke, the first thing he said was, "This is every parent's nightmare." My heart went out to him. I could feel his grief as well as my own. I told Garrett at the time that I couldn't go through the grief that Kyle's parents and family were experiencing. He understood. He was feeling it, too. Garrett went to Kyle's house and visited his mother quite often. Kyle had drawn a picture for me, and Garrett took it to his mother because she didn't have any of his art. Garrett framed a picture of Kyle snowboarding and kept it in his room. He wrote about him on his Myspace page:

Who I'd like to meet:

> unfortunately, a year ago on june 23rd a lost one of my best friends Kyle Austin Brown...one of the most talented kids i have ever met in my entire life from snowboarding to drawing flowers KB was the man... unfortunately Kyy left but only to belong in a beautiful place ....m...e...e.... .e.......... 1 L ....O ....V .... E

Kyle's passing saddened all of us who knew him, but it was a big blow to Garrett.

In the late summer of 2005, Garrett and I were driving through the small town of Wilsonville, Oregon, when we came upon a young man holding up a sign requesting food. It was a hot afternoon and there was a lot of traffic, but Garrett insisted we bring this guy some food. I said to him, "How do you know he's not trying to scam people?" Garrett replied, "Mom, he just wants food." How could I argue with that? Garrett wanted to go to his favorite burger place. "I know just what to get him," he said and ordered all his favorites. We had a big bag of food, drinks, and shakes and drove around and found the guy. I slowed down so Garrett could give him the food. That was Garrett, a heart of gold.

Chapter Nine

New Beginning and Completion

Trust thyself, every heart vibrates to that iron string.
Accept the place the divine providence has found for you,
the society of your contemporaries, the connection
of events, Great men have always done so.
—Ralph Waldo Emerson

We sold our dream home in Stafford. I was melancholy. My desires for our lives were not going to happen as I had planned. My wish for Garrett to get married at our Stafford home was not going to happen. It was going to take some time for new dreams to form. I went through the motions of physically moving forward. I found a home for us in a little suburb east of Portland called Happy Valley. Even though Garrett preferred to stay in the Stafford area, he loved our new house. It was a traditional cozy home in a family neighborhood—three bedrooms, good-sized yard for the dogs, walking paths throughout the neighborhood, good schools and location. It met all my requirements.

It took me about a year to get my bearings back on track. I was determined to move forward and begin a new career. What career I wasn't exactly sure. I had experience working for myself. I liked consulting, and I knew I could do some event marketing, although that topic didn't really excite me. Nonetheless, I had a clean slate and was looking forward to discovering what was next.

While I was regrouping, there were still rumblings with Ryan's father. Even though we were divorced, there were signs that warranted my concern for Ryan's well-being while in his father's care. They escalated throughout the year, causing me to seek legal counsel. What ensued was even more stressful than the divorce. I discovered the woman who was living with him was also an alcoholic. Initially, there was nothing I could do legally about sending my two-year-old off with two alcoholics who had no intention of being sober. This left me feeling frustrated and powerless. Several things happened within a short period of time. I learned that the woman living with Josh had three consecutive DUIs in the previous ninety days and was not allowed to be alone with her own three children. I was furious that Josh would put Ryan in the care of someone in this condition, which told me he was completely gone. While we were lawyering about this, they got married. When was this ever going to end? Sometimes there is no common sense in the legal system. Legally, I couldn't stop Josh from taking Ryan, but I did. I allowed only supervised visits. I was not willing to send a two-year-old off with them. What parent in his or her right mind would? I seemed to forget that I could choose peace when dealing in this arena. Things eventually worked out. His wife was sent to jail; he said he was getting a divorce; and we worked out an agreement.

In every other area of my life, things were moving forward and falling into place. During the year following the divorce, I took classes on spiritual development. I was determined to understand myself better and not find myself in a similar situation again. Garrett and I were close. He was a good brother to Ryan, spending time playing with him. Ryan didn't speak much until he was about three. He loved playing with Garrett and followed him around the house. He couldn't say "Garrett," but he called him G. He was an easygoing little boy, very bright. He did well in preschool and enjoyed it. Garrett and his friends would come over, and it felt good to have the kids over at the house. Things were feeling normal.

About seven months before Garrett transitioned, he had taken some hallucinogenic mushrooms with friends and had a mystical experience. It changed him. When he described part of his experience, he had told me that he had seen fear. He saw fears that he wasn't aware that he had. He saw the fears of other people, too, how most of us are living in fear and how fear runs our lives. This experience had evolved him to a place spiritually that I had not yet experienced. He shared with me that he could walk down the street and feel the oneness with the trees. He understood there is a oneness, and we are all connected.

Garrett was greatly changed after this experience, and he wanted to better understand it and himself. After his friend Kyle had passed, Garrett met a counselor/shaman who had offered to help Garrett process his grief. Garrett didn't take him up on this offer until after his mystical experience.

He knew that Stan would be able to help him make sense of his experience and Kyle's passing. Garrett worked with Stan for several months; he gave Garrett tools and spiritual guidance.

For his nineteenth birthday, Garrett wanted to spend time alone camping. The day before his birthday, I drove him up to a spot in the Columbia River Gorge. The Columbia River separates Oregon and Washington. The land was Native American. There are many waterfalls, hiking trails, and camping. It's a beautiful area with large cliffs and fir trees everywhere.

It was March and still cold and rainy with patches of snow on the ground. Garrett had his pack, and our dog Chico went with him. We thought BJ was too old to go. I agreed to pick him up the next afternoon on his birthday. After Garrett's transition, I found his notebook. This is what he wrote about his experience:

> So oh my God...I finally got settled after I set camp, it started raining very hard and I realized all the wood around me was soaked. I noticed a crevice, half cave across the 20 yard creek. I packed my bag half assed and put stuff in my sleeping bag and decided to descend across the freezing water. I prayed that I would not fall. I got across fine except my feet were soooo cold. Then I realized Chico hadn't made it across. I could tell she was very scared even though the deepest part was maybe up to my thighs. I called her and called her many times, she kept trying and turning back. I knew I was going to have to recross then carry her back. My toes finally starting to warm back up, I went back across, my feet were about to fall off, I got across just fine. I waited about one minute, picked her up and started going back again, about three quarters of the way I tripped and dropped her. I could tell she was so scared she was dog paddling with all her might. I grabbed her collar and guided her as she swam. We finally got on land. My legs and feet were so red from the freezing water it kind of scared me. After I unpacked I called Chris (my wolf) I talked to him for a while and he made me comfortable. I then cooked lunch or dinner (I'm not sure yet). My phone's clock is not working like I thought it would. I did the ritual Stan taught me and it also felt very good and soothing. I'm just so happy, so free, so alive it's just amazing. I am just going to chill and stay warm. I have a concern about Chico staying warm but I believe she will be fine. Plus I got a plan for that too!!

On the cover of his notebook, he wrote, "I have accomplished what I was searching for."

Several months later, Garrett told me that he had recently taken LSD, and he was having profound experiences. I shared my concerns about LSD to Garrett and encouraged him to talk to Stan for guidance. He was researching his experiences and called and talked to me about his findings. He had discovered Timothy Leary's work and connected with it. Like many people on a spiritual path, he was excited. He had spiritual information he wanted to share with others.

I was concerned about his taking LSD. I'd never tried it. It was a drug that always scared me. What did help was that I had read references about it in some of the spiritual texts I had been reading—not in a way to encourage anyone to take it, but referencing experiences. So, at the time he talked to me about it, I was probably the most open that I could be on the subject.

I really didn't want to share Garrett's experience with LSD in this book because I didn't want people to judge Garrett. However, his friends encouraged me to share it. I was told to tell it all, and I am. Of course I know it's what Garrett wants. He was pushing me to share, and that's why there was so much encouragement from his peers. It's a part of his path, and there really is nothing wrong with it. And, OK, it also helped that I read *Steve Jobs* by Walter Isaacson. In the book, Steve shared that when he was about Garrett's age, he used LSD. He said, "Our consciousness was raised by Zen, and also by LSD." Even later in life, he would credit psychedelic drugs for making him more enlightened:

> Taking LSD was a profound experience, one of the most important things in my life. LSD shows you that there's another side to the coin, and you can't remember when it wears off, but you know it. It reinforced my sense of what was important—creating great things instead of making money, putting things back into the stream of history and of human consciousness as much as I could.

Garrett also shared from this experience he knew the cure for AIDS, and when I asked him, "What is it?" he said, "Love." I knew what he meant, and I was blown away that a nineteen-year-old was sharing this with me. That he had this kind of understanding I was just beginning to grasp.

I had been reading different spiritual texts and teachings, which were saying the same thing—that if we truly loved ourselves and others, there would be no disease. I had read that the word disease broken down is dis - ease, meaning, not of ease.

He shared he understood how I tried to help him when he was growing up. He said, "Mom, I get it now. When I was younger, I only saw what was in front of me, but you could see the bigger picture and there is always a bigger picture." It was music to my ears. He understood where I had been coming from. When he shared this, there was a grace that was palpable.

For years, Garrett had been interested in becoming a cinematographer. He often had a camera with him and loved filming. He particularly liked filming snowboarding and was often watching a current snowboard DVD. He had applied and, to his excitement, had been accepted at the Portland Art Institute. At the last minute, though, he decided not to attend. Right before he passed, Garrett said that he wanted to change his career direction, which surprised me because he was so creative. Working with some sort of art medium, whether it be film, drawing, or music, fit him so well. Creativity was a big part of who he was.

During this conversation, which was about two weeks before Garrett transitioned, he told me that he had a message to share, and he wanted to begin taking psychology courses. This complete change in career direction had surprised me, but I supported him. I had done the same thing years earlier and had always told him to follow his heart. To be taken seriously, he told me, he was going to need credentials. He knew he would sound crazy if he didn't have a credible education before sharing what he experienced.

I didn't know that Garrett had been talking to friends about his spiritual awakening. To him, the LSD was a way to connect with Spirit, and he was encouraging others to try it as well. He so wanted others to feel and understand what he had experienced. There were a few of his friends who were having the same experiences and understood what he wanted for them. Others were wondering if he was losing his grasp on reality.

Garrett and I had had a disagreement the last time I saw him in his physical form. He was not happy with me. A few days before Garrett passed he had called me to get Stan's phone number. I was so relieved that he'd called for it. I knew he was going to be OK. I trusted that Stan would help him with his spiritual awakening and guide him away from the LSD and back to the experiences he'd had in nature.

In hindsight, there were many things that had happened. He and Josh seemed to have reconciled their relationship, and he reconnected with people he hadn't talked to in a while. The conversations we'd had, how close we had been—as I reflect on it now, it makes sense that he would transition. About two to three weeks before he left his body, I told him about a book I was reading about telepathy, communicating without calling each other. Garrett and I were in the process of trying this when he transitioned. How incredible! We were already beginning to communicate with him not being physically present. I had no idea that, soon, it would be our regular mode of communication.

Right before he passed, Garrett shared a sweet experience. When we were talking on the phone one afternoon, he told me about a recent hot summer afternoon on a crowded bus. A grandmotherly Vietnamese woman boarded and didn't seem to understand English. The bus driver was telling her how much she needed to pay, but she didn't understand and was clearly upset. Garrett said that he helped her get the right amount of bus fare for her ride. He shared with me the compassion he felt for her in this situation, how he was happy that he could help her in such a simple way.

A few months before his passing, I had written a vision of my life. In part of it, Garrett and I were working on a nonprofit together. I shared my vision with Garrett and that I knew someday we would do a nonprofit together. Before his transition, he was working on a nonprofit he wanted to start. It was something he hadn't yet shared with me.

I always felt there was a purpose for my being in Manhattan on September 11, 2001. I began to look at the event symbolically. This shift in perspective helped me to better understand unwanted events in my own life. I realized for the new to come in, the old had to go out. I see this pattern in my life, with friends and with clients. Understanding the event in this way helped me as I was rebuilding my life. Recognizing that the change was an opportunity for the growth I'd been asking for all along. To resist it would keep away the things I really wanted.

While I was doing my Soul searching, discovering my next career was a primary focus. A couple of friends had suggested life coaching, but I didn't take it seriously until it came up a third time. I had learned that when something comes around a third time, pay attention! I did my due diligence and realized coaching was a perfect fit. It was as if everything in my life had been preparing me for this work. To put it simply, I love learning and growing. It's what interests me. I've always been passionate about learning and change. Coaching fulfilled the depth of work that had been calling me for years; it was time to let it in.

I found a program with an excellent reputation in Bellevue, Washington. After interviewing graduates and the founder, I decided the program was a good fit. I could make the three-hour drive to Bellevue, take classes over long weekends. It was challenging with all the legal stress and drama going on with Ryan's dad. I remember a time receiving disappointing news from my lawyer and after class breaking down in tears over the stress of it all. While I was out of town, I feared Ryan's dad would find out I was in Bellevue and try to take him. This never happened, but nonetheless I worried that it would. I worried constantly and feared for Ryan's safety and well-being.

I completed the rigorous coaching program and received credentialing as a professional coach. Taking all I had learned from my professional experience in high technology—along with my consulting practice and, most important, my spiritual growth—I launched a coaching practice focused on career transition and leadership development. I felt revitalized. I was excited about my life and future and so was Garrett.

In 2006 I began thinking about September 11 again, and I had a strong pull to be at Ground Zero on the fifth anniversary. Through a series of surprising events, I ended up going with a coaching colleague. At the time we barely knew each other, but there was a special connection. We both could feel it, so we both trusted it and went.

Anna had never been to New York. We were excited to see how the trip would unfold. While we couldn't get in to the anniversary ceremony, as it was only for family and dignitaries, we did find a place across the street with many others and listened as each family member spoke the name of the loved one who had passed as a result of the event. I sat with my eyes closed most of the time, sending love to each person as he or she spoke. I could feel the pain of each person. Most said a little something more than the name of the loved one. I noticed that as each person spoke, it was as if the event had just happened. Discerning their grief, it didn't seem like five years had passed. The grief sounded fresh. My heart went out to them. I also felt my own sadness about the ending of my marriage. I had always felt that the man I married had died, and somehow being in attendance was helpful in my moving forward. After we went on that trip, I was at peace with my emotions about September 11. Whatever had been lingering had its completion.

Just as the life I was rebuilding was coming together, everything changed. I had my own Twin Towers crash down, and I would never be the same again.

Chapter Ten

Worst Nightmare Comes True

It's a force that appears to be negative, but actually
shows you how to realize your Personal Legend.
It prepares your spirit and your will, because there is one
great truth on this planet: whoever you are, or whatever it is
that you do, when you really want something, it's because
that desire originated in the soul of the universe.
It's your mission on earth.
—Paulo Coelho, The Alchemist

Since September 11, the world has been different. Almost everyone uses the barometer pre- and post-9/11. For several years I used a similar measurement in my life. Things were pre- or post-October 21, 2006, Garrett's transition day.

On Friday, October 20, 2006, Ryan and I took a weekend trip to Bend, a small resort town in central Oregon about three hours east of Portland. It was a beautiful fall weekend—sunny and still warm, an Indian summer. On the drive over, I called and left a message with Kelly, a close friend of Garrett's, to see if she and Garrett wanted to go to the pumpkin patch with me and Ryan when we returned to Portland.

After arriving in Bend, I took Ryan to the park to play after the long car ride. Ryan was playing on the playground when I began experiencing a tightness in my chest. At the time, I was contemplating more changes in my life, and I thought it might be due to this thought process. As the day went on and into the evening, the pain persisted. After dinner we went to our hotel, and I put Ryan to bed. I was lying in bed reading a book, and my chest was still bothering me. It was a tightness I had never felt before.

It was quite different from the running anxiety I felt after September 11. Even though I was in perfect heath, I was getting concerned and wondered if I was going to have a heart attack. When we returned home on Sunday, I was still experiencing this tightness in my chest.

The next evening after I had put Ryan to bed, I received a call from Garrett's friend Kelly. She asked me if I had seen or talked to Garrett over the weekend. I told her I had not. She was concerned because she hadn't either. She had been calling around, but no one had seen Garrett or talked to him since Friday night. Over the summer, Garrett had been dating a girl in Eugene, and I suggested that Garrett might have gone to Eugene to visit friends. But Kelly was clearly worried and suggested I call the police. Her urgency had come out of nowhere.

"Is there something I should know? Is Garrett in some kind of trouble?" I asked.

"It's nothing like that," she'd told me. "It's just that other friends of Garrett's have been looking for him all day, and no one can find him."

Then Kelly said something quite startling. "Dana, there was a report on the news a young man had been hit by a train. I'm afraid it might be Garrett."

I was sure that it was not, but Kelly was persistent. To appease her, I told her I would call the police department, which I immediately did, still not thinking it could be Garrett. When I reached the police department, they wanted me to talk to the medical examiner, so they transferred my call. The medical examiner told me the person was a young man in his early twenties. I explained to him that no one had seen my son over the weekend, but I didn't think the person they had was my son because he was only nineteen. The medical examiner then described the clothes the person was wearing. I fixated on the shoes—he said this person was wearing brown Vans. Garrett didn't have brown Vans, so I knew it couldn't be him. Then, he said the young man had a distinct tattoo on his right arm. Garrett had just gotten a tattoo in honor of Kyle, who passed the year before. It was a unique tattoo Garrett had specially designed. When I described the tattoo, he said to me, "I think we've got your boy." He told me there was a picture of the tattoo on the local news website. They did not want to show it on TV because they hadn't wanted the family to see it before they were notified. The medical examiner said, "This person didn't have any identification on him." Garrett often forgot his ID.

Although I was shaken after talking to the medical examiner, I still wasn't convinced it was Garrett. I couldn't bring myself to look up the website, so I called Kevin and told him what had happened. He told me he had seen the story on the news, and it wasn't Garrett. Apparently over the weekend, there were two different people hit by trains. Still, I had his dad look up the website, and from the other end of the phone I heard, "Oh my God."

That was it. I was gone.

There it was. My worst fear had happened. Not that I would die, but that Garrett would leave before me.

When I began to comprehend that Garrett had passed, I immediately left my body. I could see myself crumpled up on the kitchen floor, crying, and a part of me was watching this scene.

The year that was to follow was the most turbulent I had ever experienced. It was anything but a quiet year of grief. It was a hold-on-to-your-hat kind of year because everything I had once known was going to be under scrutiny. I was going to look at my life very honestly and deeply—a new way of being was becoming within in me.

During the first year of Garrett's passing, many things were happening all at once. The period immediately following Garrett's transition was obviously emotional; just comprehending that he had really left his body was overwhelming. I still had a lingering belief that it wasn't true. I was struggling because I had felt him so powerfully. Over the past few years, I had garnered new beliefs that were now being put to the test. What I really believed, based on how I was thinking and feeling, was becoming clear. Being a coach, my natural tendency was challenging myself: If I really believe Garrett is here and connecting with me, why am I feeling this badly? Why do I allow myself these thoughts that don't feel good to me?

I would vacillate between the old fears and my knowing that I was getting stronger. There were times of great clarity, but in the beginning I couldn't always hold on to it.

Assimilating Garrett's transition and my life was my internal work. I struggled with what I thought were contradictions. At times I felt like I was in a paper bag and someone was shaking it. It was dark and I felt disoriented. What came of this process was a strong desire for connection and peace from the deepest levels of my being.

I want to share the major events during the first year after Garrett's transition because their culmination led me to where I am now. Although the experiences were uniquely mine, you, too, have a culmination of events in your life that have led you to where you are in this moment. Reflection is invaluable for making changes and moving forward. Dwelling is dangerous; it keeps you in the past and away from growth.

Everyone we loved and who loved us was present to us. I could feel it. I knew that prayers helped people, but this was the first time I knowingly felt them. Never have I felt so much love, so strong a feeling of being held. It was during this time that I could see and feel angels beside me. It was a great comfort.

Family, friends—both mine and Garrett's—filled my house for quite some time after Garrett's passing. Sometimes I felt strong and connected with my son; other times, I felt disconnected and victimized. Why Garrett? Out of all the people in the world, why did it have to be him? My boy. Why?

Everyone loved Garrett. He was charismatic. He had so much love for everyone and life. His passing didn't make any sense to me at the time. It was difficult to get my head around the fact he had transitioned—not only that, but in what felt like such a random way, being hit by a train. And yet, in a strange way, that would be Garrett.

Someone brought some of Garrett's clothes home, and as I was going through them I saw one of his favorite shirts. I bought it for him when we went shopping together. We both loved it. I thought of how handsome he looked when he wore it. It was a long-sleeved, button-down Ralph Lauren shirt with narrow pink, white, and green vertical stripes. It smelled like him. I immediately put it on over the shirt I was wearing. I wore it over my shirts, unbuttoned like a sweater, like Garrett hugging me, every day for weeks. After a long while, I finally washed it and then slept in it for months. I also began wearing the pink plastic ring Garrett had given me ten years earlier. It was a reminder of his love.

Though I was inclined to have Garrett cremated, I wavered at first. With every decision I was in the habit of asking myself, *What would Garrett want?* I was talking to Garrett's friend, Lauren, and she had reminded me that when Garrett's friend Kyle passed, Garrett had collapsed when he saw Kyle in a casket. He had told her then he wanted to be cremated. So, that was done. Garrett had already made that decision.

It took a day or so to get things sorted out with the medical examiner's office and move Garrett's body to a nearby funeral home. There were conversations with the police on what had happened. It was determined an accident; no one else was with him. He was hit on Saturday, around five in the morning. Details about what had happened were coming together. I immediately remembered my chest pain, which began Friday afternoon. I knew this pain was directly related to Garrett. On some level, I was connected to what was going to happen, and I felt it in my heart—where Garrett resides. Not once over the weekend was I worried about him, but on a Soul level I knew.

I agonized whether to have a private viewing of Garrett. In the end, I couldn't put him in a casket. The embalming process didn't feel right. It all seemed unnatural to me and invasive. Being in my not-so-rational mind, I didn't want to hurt Garrett or do anything that he wouldn't choose. I couldn't imagine him embalmed in a casket in a funeral home; that was not Garrett. None of my immediate family members were up to seeing Garrett's body. His father and his older brother could not bring themselves to see Garrett's body, which I completely understood. Recalling Kyle's funeral the year before, his friends were so young, and I felt it might be too traumatic for them. In truth, it would have been traumatic for all of us. Garrett embodied life, freedom, love, peace, and nature. All these things considered, there was no viewing.

At first I wasn't sure if I could see Garrett's body either. Some said it would be too upsetting, too painful. My dear friend Roxanne, whom I've known since first grade, and her mother, Alice, had come to see me, bless their hearts. When I opened the front door, it was like seeing two angels standing in front of me. Both Roxanne's sister and brother had passed, and we talked about seeing Garrett's body. Alice told me that she had kissed her children good-bye, and I knew that's what I wanted to do. I wanted to kiss my son again one last time. I am grateful we had that conversation. It was comforting speaking to another mother who had been in my shoes. Alice knew exactly what I was feeling, and Roxanne had had the experience of both her siblings, with whom she was very close, pass. If they had not shown up in that perfect moment, I might not have had one of the most profound experiences of my life.

The funeral home was located near my house on Mt. Scott. It was a beautiful fall day, I remember, and the grounds where stunning with fall foliage. I was thinking Garrett would love the beauty, especially the trees. My experience with Garrett in the funeral home was both surreal and grounding. When I saw his body, it was him—there was no mistake. But it didn't look like him. He was on a gurney with blankets over his body, and his head was exposed. Garrett looked as if he were lying on a hospital bed.

I kissed his cheek. It was cold, no Garrett energy there. His body was no longer animated. His consciousness was no longer residing there. His body was no more than a shell because that part of him—that life force that made that body Garrett—was no longer there.

For a moment the situation got a little dizzying, as I strongly felt him. His energy was palpable. I knew it was him; I could literally feel him. The energy right above me was unmistakable. It was an extremely surreal moment. I was still in shock that he had transitioned. Psychologically, it was difficult for me to absorb. Standing before my beautiful son's body, clearly he was not there, and yet I could feel his presence. I sat in a chair a few feet from him and could feel his energy right above my head. It was the same energy I'd felt the night he was born.

It was an overwhelming love, and I recognized it instantly as I sat with him. I hadn't thought about the energy in the hospital room in years, but in that moment I remembered.

When I first walked into the room, I was traumatized, in shock. But after I felt Garrett's energy, I felt peaceful—and a strength within me I didn't know existed. Without my saying a word, we talked, even though I was sobbing. I could hear his thoughts directed at me. The knowing I felt is hard to explain. He was with me, and he was doing everything in his power to talk to me, to let me know he was near and OK. Most of all, he wanted me to know how much he loved me and appreciated me being his mother. He wanted me to know that I was a good mother. He knew it was important for me to know. I so badly wanted to be a good mother, and he was telling me I was. His message, delivered with love, was the message I wanted to hear the most. He knew it and didn't hold back. When I left I had clarity, and I felt peaceful and strong. It was a blessing, an experience I'll always remember.

During this time, I was remembering when Garrett would visit Kyle's parents after Kyle passed. I thought of that picture Kyle had drawn for me that Garrett gave Kyle's mother. I was so glad he had done that for her; it was bittersweet.

Somewhere in all of this, the topic of an obituary came up. I could not bring myself to say the word. I completely resisted it; instead, I referred to it as Garrett's Story. I wrote Garrett's Story, completely from my heart. When I reread it, I thought Garrett would say, "It sounds like my mother wrote it." I asked Josh if he would read it and give me some feedback. He did and to my surprise he thought it was perfect. I included a picture of Garrett in the wilderness. His smile in the picture said it all.

A group of Garrett's close friends flew up from Tahoe and stayed with me and attended the celebration that we had planned for Garrett. We noticed signs that were from Garrett. The computer would change screens, or a certain song would play. The water in the downstairs bathroom would often be running, even though no one had been in the bathroom. Garrett gave us these signs for weeks. We all felt Garrett's presence, knowing he was trying to comfort us and let us know he was with us. Having the boys in my home was a relief—their energy and love and the stories they shared. There was a lot of laughter and tears. It was bittersweet and so important for all of us in our grief process.

Another friend, Joe, came by one day with several items of Garrett's, one of which was his driver's license. He had retrieved it from where Garrett had left it and surprised me with it. He also gave me the most recent CD Garrett had burned and was listening to. It was an eclectic mix, from hard rock to country and everything in between. I listened to that CD over and over. I had it playing in the background for quite a while. It connected me to him. The first track on it was his recent favorite song, which he had shared with me, *Smiley Faces* by Gnarls Barkley. The second track was an old song I had never heard before: *Wish You Were Here* by Pink Floyd. I thought he was listening to the song because it was how he felt about his friend Kyle. It took on a deeper meaning when my niece Brittany asked me if I had listened to the lyrics. Then, I felt as if Garrett was talking to me through the song:

So, so you think you can tell
Heaven from Hell,
Blue skies from pain.
Can you tell a green field
From a cold steel rail?
A smile from a veil?
Do you think you can tell?

Until Joe brought the CD over, I had never heard the song. Since then, I've heard it playing many times while I'm shopping in stores.

I was proud of all Garrett's friends. They showed up for him and his family, like Garrett would have done for any of them. It was a spectacular show of love.

For several days after Garrett passed, John, a friend of mine and Garrett's, had tried to reach Stan. I received a call at about five in the morning several days after Garrett passed. It was Stan. He told me he had been in Taos and outside cell coverage. He had just come down the mountain and received the messages. He told me while he was on the mountain, he did receive some guidance that something had happened to a son. Stan had wondered if it was his own son. He also told me that Garrett had left a message for him, but they had missed each other. This gave me great comfort, and later I wondered, if they would have connected, would the outcome have been the same? Stan is not only a shaman but an angel to Garrett and me. He went out of his way for Garrett. He stayed an extra day, and he went to the El Santuario de Chimayo, a small chapel in Santa

Fe known as the Lourdes of America. This is where Stan performed a special ceremony for Garrett and brought back a candle and cross from this sacred space, which he gave to me.

Josh and a couple of Garrett's friends shared that Garrett was in the process of starting a nonprofit. Garrett had an idea inspired by a place he liked to go that was downtown. It was a coffee bar, with computer gaming, board games, and local art. He loved going downtown and hanging out there. It had a very eclectic feel. I had picked Garrett up from this place several times and knew he really liked being there. I wasn't aware that it inspired him to want to start a nonprofit for high school and college-age kids. Garrett had wanted a safe place where they could come and hang out and be who they are. He wanted it to be a coffee bar with snacks with healthy alternatives. He wanted a place where kids could go to find resources for jobs, to discover who they are. I was surprised and not surprised. I was encouraged to start this for Garrett. Even though I was quite overwhelmed at the time and didn't know emotionally how I could begin a project like this, I decided I wanted to do it for and with Garrett. With Josh's help I applied for the nonprofit, Garrett's Space.

It was a beautiful fall—sunny and unusually dry for the Pacific Northwest. It had been sunny every day for weeks until this day, Saturday, November 4, 2006. This Saturday, it began to rain a true Pacific-Northwest downpour. We were in a big, white tent located in the Mt. Hood National Forest at the base of the mountain Garrett loved to snowboard on, where he'd spent several summers at snowboard camp. It was the perfect location.

Friends and loved ones arrived as expected; my brother brought BJ, Garrett's beloved dog. Everything about the celebration was carefully chosen. It was important to me that the celebration felt like Garrett; it had to be like him. His friend Stan was there to do a Pushing Ceremony for Garrett. We had canvases for everyone to sign and information regarding Garrett's nonprofit. Donations were appreciated in lieu of flowers. There was a video montage of Garrett with his favorite songs playing on a big screen and a bonfire to follow the Pushing Ceremony. Garrett loved bonfires. Garrett's shirt, jeans, and shoes were present for the ceremony, along with his ashes inside his Burton backpack that he had carried around since he was twelve-years-old (he wasn't the urn type).

Everyone was there, including Garrett. I could feel him. I felt him at every step in planning his celebration.

A close friend said she didn't know how I could possibly speak at this event. I did not know how I could *not* speak. During the days following his transition, I could muster a strength that was baffling, even to me. At times, I had amazing clarity and knowing.

We were all present to celebrate Garrett, to celebrate his light—in love and many tears. There were many familiar faces, some I hadn't seen in many years. I was surprised at how many were there for Garrett whom I had never met. Some had never met Garrett but were present in support of us. Garrett loved trees, and a friend of my dear friend who had a Christmas tree farm donated seedling trees so that everyone who attended received a seedling tree to take home and plant in honor of Garrett.

I talked about Garrett and his light, but I remember talking mostly about what events like this mean to us, for those of us who are feeling we have lost our son, brother, grandson, best friend, cousin, nephew. I remember talking about what it means when we are faced with a major jolt. It is our opportunity for transformation, not just Garrett's. Heaven has ways of speaking to us, and this was clearly an opportunity for each of us to look within and discover our own awakening. This did not need to be a tragedy. Garrett would never want that. He would want all of us to know the eternalness he was experiencing. How I came up with this at the time, I don't know, but something inside me knew.

I spoke first, then Kevin, then Josh, and then two of Garrett's close friends, Kelly and Lauren. The microphone was open to anyone else who was inspired to share. Mostly his peers spoke, sharing story after story about how Garrett touched them in a special way. I realized how special Garrett made others feel. Many felt that Garrett was their best friend.

When all had been said, Stan led us in a Pushing Ceremony, which was powerful. He had us seated in a V formation with Garrett's clothes and his ashes that were in his backpack at the front. Directly behind his things were Garrett's family and friends. Stan led us in a song, giving us the words while he drummed; it was beautiful. I felt completely buoyed by the energy rushing through me toward Garrett. I felt a similar energy when the angels held me, but it was even stronger. It moved not only around me but through me. It was quite an emotional experience. In essence everyone there was pushing Garrett's energy up to the heavens. It was beautiful. Garrett loved it, I knew.

Chapter Eleven

Dark Days

Many of us spend our whole lives running from feeling with the mistaken belief that you can not bear the pain. But you have already borne the pain. What you have not done is feel you are beyond that pain.
—Kahlil Gibran

Thank God for my friends, Garrett's friends, and my family for being there to support me and Ryan. My sister was incredible; she helped me in any and every way, especially with Ryan. The coaching community reached out to me, and the support I received from these colleagues was generous, full of compassion and wisdom. The friends who connected me with other mothers who had been in my shoes were a blessing. Having support was helpful, but even that had to ease up, and eventually it was me and Ryan.

I was a roller coaster of emotions, from feeling strong and connected to being a complete mess. For a while, I was numb, in shock, and went through the motion of what had to get done next. I spent time in counsel with Stan. I wanted to be strong. What this really meant was that I was afraid to allow my feelings. I remember Stan telling me it was OK to cry and grieve. I remember him saying, "Dana, even the Dalai Lama would cry." I told him, "I'm afraid if I start, I won't come back from it." He reassured me that that would not happen. Because I was healthy, he said, I would come through it, and I believed him.

I made a conscious decision to allow myself to grieve. Even though I really did not want to do it, it was an important step so that I could go forward. My internship training at The Dougy Center had taught me this, and Stan encouraged it. I decided to take the next few months, or as long as it would take, to grieve and take care of Ryan. Really, it's all I had the capacity to do anyway. I had just started my career coaching practice earlier in the year, and I decided it could be put on hold for a while. I was fortunate that financially I was able to take the time off. It ended up being almost four months before I began to work again. It was a gift to have had this time.

During these months, I started my day by getting up, getting dressed, getting Ryan ready, and taking him to preschool. After I dropped him off, I would go back home, get in my bathrobe, lay around, cry, and not much else until I had to get dressed to pick up Ryan from preschool at two o'clock. Then, the rest of the day I tried to have some order of normalcy for Ryan's sake.

There were times when Ryan was not home, and I would stand in the shower and scream and cry in despair. I couldn't stand that Garrett wasn't in his body. Nor could I handle the thought of no connection with Garrett. I would think, He's gone. And it would kill me inside. I couldn't bear the feeling of emptiness such thoughts gave me. I felt completely empty inside, and at times I thought I would go crazy from the grief. In these moments, I could feel no spiritual connection, and it would scare me. I wanted to understand why this had happened to my boy. I could not have felt more like a victim, completely powerless and in despair.

I spent many days thinking about how my whole life had changed, wondering how people could do things like go grocery shopping. Others' lives were moving forward, but mine had completely stopped. It was difficult to focus on anything but Garrett being gone. Nothing seemed to matter. The little things that seemed important were no longer important. I could see how most things that I and most others worry about are so trivial in the big picture. They are just energy wasters; they really don't matter. I spent time reflecting, remembering everything I could about Garrett from when he was a baby until he passed. I wanted to remember everything. I wished I would have spent more time with him, even though we spent much time together.

My friend Angie was a lifeline. We had many heartfelt conversations on the phone when our children were napping. We would talk about angels. She would always let me know when a medium was going to be on TV, and we would discuss it. Our conversations became one of the first things I began to look forward to in my day. Those times we spent were simple and sacred, having my dear friend speak to me heart to heart, mother to mother. Her friendship was the perfect example of compassion. She never said anything that would insinuate in any way I was a victim in what had happened. She wouldn't allow me to go there.

Even with all the love and support, I was going to have to do my own work. No one could do it for me. This reminds me of something my spiritual guide shared with me while I was in the middle of my divorce with Ryan's father. He said, "Dana, it's always between you and God." I certainly wasn't alone, but I had to find a way to surrender and make peace with Garrett's passing.

There was a pivotal moment, when I was giving Ryan a bath. I was watching my beautiful three-year-old boy, happy and splashing in the water without a care in the world, like a normal three-year-old. And I was a grieving mother just wanting to leave so I could be with Garrett. Looking at beautiful Ryan, I realized that he needed me; he really needed me. If I wasn't here, he would be with his father, and his father was in no condition to take care of Ryan. It was in that moment I made the decision that I wanted to feel better. I wanted to be here, to be present and feel joy again with Ryan. I think Ryan's being here saved me. He came into my life at the perfect time. He is a gift from heaven.

Chapter Twelve

What Happened?

When the soul returns to itself and reflects,
it passes into the region of that which is
pure and everlasting, immortal and unchangeable.
—Plato, Phaedo

The mystery of the brown Vans was revealed shortly after we discovered Garrett had passed. He had borrowed the shoes from his friend. Of course, people wanted to know what happened. Although it hadn't occurred to me, I became aware that some people were wondering if Garrett had committed suicide or had been a victim of foul play. Who gets hit by a train, right? I guess these were logical questions, but they never entered my mind.

Originally, I assumed Garrett must have taken LSD because he was intrigued by mystical experiences. I later learned he loved walking along the railroad tracks. My niece Brittany shared this with me, and Kelly also knew this about him. He had also mentioned to me that he had recently been at the train station.

We had two toxicology reports completed, and both indicated he had no drugs in his system. This was a bit traumatic because I had told myself a story, and it wasn't true. In a way I felt like I was responding to the news of his passing again. It was reassuring that he had no drugs in his system. In my mind this news confirmed his leaving really was meant to happen. It was no fluke.

Garrett was happy when he transitioned. He had been at a rave, and I was happy knowing Garrett had been dancing because he loved music and dancing. It was comforting that he had been doing something he loved with friends in his last hours in his body.

I talked to Stan about people's concerns. He told me Garrett had had none of the signs of wanting to take his life; in fact, he had just renewed his driver's license and was in the process of starting a nonprofit and returning to school. He had many plans for his life. It never felt like there was foul play. I never got the sense of foul play. We really don't know if he was by himself. Some of his friends didn't think this was likely; others could see him being alone. There was a police investigation, and it was ruled an accident. I really think Garrett didn't hear the train. Recently, I had been underneath a bridge with a train track and did not hear the train until it was right over my head. I remembered this and feel it was no accident I had that experience, to help me understand.

At the time of his transition, Garrett was happy. He hadn't taken any mind-altering chemicals that would have confused him. In the beginning it was challenging to accept that it was just his time. I realize now that if he had not been hit by a train, it would have been a car crash, anything. For some reason, it was a train. What I do know now is that it doesn't matter. The how and details aren't the point. Knowing more would not change the outcome, and having more information would not bring any peace. That's from the outside. Peace is an inside job, always.

Remembering there are no accidents, that no mistakes are made when it's time to transition, helped me tremendously in accepting what had happened. It also gave me the peace I was seeking with the belief that nothing had gone wrong.

CHAPTER THIRTEEN

Garrett's Friends

We don't accomplish anything in this world alone...and whatever happens is the result of the whole tapestry of one's life and all the weaving of individual threads from one to another that creates something.
— Sandra Day O'Connor

As I began writing about Garrett, he asked me to ask some of his friends to share their perspective of him. I was relieved at this suggestion, being aware that it's easy for a mother to say and see the best in her son. I always love being with Garrett, of course, because I love being with my son, but it's more than that. It is his energy. Everyone enjoyed being in his presence. He had a charisma and charm, and he was just the type of person people wanted to be around. At our family gatherings, the party didn't really get started until Garrett arrived.

It's probably a bit more powerful to hear what his peers have to say about their experiences with him. I asked a few of his friends if they would be willing share any stories or thoughts, anything they felt comfortable sharing in this book. I received eager responses from his close friends:

Emilee

Garrett was a very radiant person. He was always smiling and making everyone around him happy. His personality shined and he was always rubbing off on everyone he was around to bring out the best in them. I don't ever remember hanging out with Garrett when I was in a bad mood, and if I was, that easily got turned around by his jokes. My biggest memory of him was when Myspace was around…We used to chat on Myspace ALL the time about Kelly and my ex, Timmy, and give relationship advice, and we would talk all night sometimes. We had never met though, and we talked for weeks, even months. One night I was at my ex-boyfriend's house, and Garrett came over to hang out, and after we talked for a little while, I just knew it was him. And I was like, "Are you Garrett?" He said yes, and I was like, "I'm Emi!" haha. It was so awesome just to instantly feel drawn to him and to just feel like I knew him SO well already, and having not even met him yet. That is an exact example of how powerful his personality was.

I truly felt like something was missing from the world when he passed. He was meant to be here and to show people that just being positive and happy means you're living life to the fullest. That feeling was there until I met you. I now feel like he is here to help you and Ryan grieve and to love you guys in a different way, from afar. Watch over you guys. It is so awesome to see how strong you are. It's admirable, and I'm sure once your book is out, it can be so much help to other families experiencing the same thing.

You're an amazing mother to Ryan, and I wish I could've seen you and Garrett together. You're the most caring person, and I am so happy that Lauren introduced us. I remember leaving your house for the first time, and I have never felt so much positive energy from Garrett passing as I did then. I finally felt closure with it, having you in my life. I got in the car with Lauren and was just bawling because it was so overwhelming—but in a good way.

Kelcey

When I think of Garrett, I think of a big kid. Soft, sweet, goofy, sensitive kid. When he took drugs he changed.

He had big dreams. He had a vision of a place for kids where they could go and be themselves and get guidance on their lives, a place where they could figure out who they are. He had a strong desire to do good, to help people.

Garrett was emotional and sensitive, and I felt as if he always trying to understand and figure things out.

Garrett thought he should be taking care of himself and didn't want to worry his mother. He knew she was raising his little brother and was having a difficult time with his father, and he didn't want to add more stress to her life.

Garrett was very passionate about things that interested him. When I think of Garrett, I think of him being goofy, popping in with a big smile. Garrett was full of ambition and passion. It seemed as if he had not yet learned to channel this. He had charisma for things he did and believed in. He had great ideas and I think some self-doubt. He knew things and wanted to share them; he loved to connect with people.

He was a guy you take to a party, and he would meet others there. He would seek them out; he was genuinely curious and never made enemies; he would meet others and get along.

It seemed important to him to connect and know many people.

Garrett could always sense when someone was having a difficult time. He would just come up and give people a hug. He would say anything. He didn't ask any questions, like, "What's the matter, what happened?" He just gave a hug. That was special, when Garrett would comfort me. Garrett was unselfish. You always knew you were his friend.

When I heard about what happened, I was in a state of shock. I saw a story on the news. They showed a tattoo; it was Garrett's. I was in a silent pain. I couldn't believe it and didn't want to. I didn't want to be sad because Garrett wouldn't want it.

We got in a big fight about a month before he passed (which was over something so stupid I don't even remember). The week before Garrett left us, we made up and we spent the day together down at the local town park, laughing and having a good time. Looking back that we had this day together makes me grateful and at peace. I can't imagine what I would have felt like if we didn't get to spend that last day together. This is a constant reminder to me to not hold grudges and realize how vulnerable life really is. Don't stay mad at people you care about. You just never know when your last day together will be.

At his celebration, I chose not to be sad because Garrett would never want anyone to be sad. I went to his celebration remembering all the good, because I know that is what Garrett would want.

Phil

It was strange that Garrett was hit by a train, and yet, it was, in a way, Garrett. Trains have a lot of energy, and this feels symbolic to Garrett's transition. It's been hard trying to make sense of what exactly happened that night with Garrett. I wonder what he was thinking, how he felt, what exactly happened. I talked to someone who knew him one time and, for a moment, I wondered if he knew something.

It's really hard to put into words. It's as if Garrett knew too much and had to leave.

Garrett could see how each of us has a life path, and there are specific things that we are meant to experience, the major events that happen in our lives. He had to explain this concept to me a few times before I really got it. When I did, I felt chills.

He always wanted everyone to have a good time. He would give money to people who needed it, and when we would go out he would spot people money to help them so that they could go, too.

Garrett experienced the mystical effects of LSD and wanted to share his insights of his experience with others. He was quite passionate about sharing this message. He wanted others to know what he had learned. He was passionate about sharing his insights on our lives being guided. When you take LSD, it's hard to explain what it's like to others, but it is like seeing through God's eyes.

Garrett talked about being able to have the same feelings as when you take LSD, but without having to take it. You could go back to the memory of it and feel the feelings of it.

"Closely connected," he would often say to me, "You know what I mean?" And I completely understood him; we didn't need words. We both understood and knew. We understood and communicated without words. We were on the same wavelength. It really was all about peace and love. We spent a lot of time together; he was always around. We were close, closer than brothers. There was no judgment, almost like a parent relationship in that he was wise. Recently, one of my professors was explaining that only five percent of the population develop wisdom, a complete understanding of what life is really about. When he left, there was this loss. Other than my mother, I really didn't have anyone I could talk to about it.

He would share what he knew, and there were people who just didn't understand where he was coming from and thought he had lost it. It's hard to understand if you have not had the experience.

Lauren

Garrett will always be my older brother who brought my soul to where I belonged all along: Tahoe. Garrett will always be my best friend; no matter what he does, I can't be mad when he smiles. Garrett will always be my guardian angel who has guided me to success by taking chances. Garrett is also a connector who has led me to some of the most amazing friends I've had in life. But most of all...Garrett was Garrett, and no one can ever take that away.

Jesse

Garrett Michael Kyle was one of the most interesting, amazing, heartwarming people I have ever met in my life. His energy, spunk, and personality in general were beyond any other I have ever encountered.

Garrett and I started as enemies actually. It was back in eighth grade at Kingsbury Middle School. We got into an altercation because of a basketball game. We argued and pushed one another. Ever since then, we were not cool with each other. Then a younger girl in seventh grade told Garrett I hit her so he would purposely try to fight me. See, in middle school, kids are horribly mean to one another. Kids lie, steal, cheat, and do horrible things to each other. Other kids were purposely trying to get us to fight simply because they wanted to see a fight. Garrett and I never fought. It came to an end when a teacher started to notice we had problems with each other. Garrett and I never spoke the rest of the year in fear we both would get into trouble. It doesn't end there, sadly. In our beginning years of high school at George Whittell, Garrett and I ran into another altercation when we both were questioned by the seniors at the time, who egged one of their houses. Garrett and I were somehow both together in the locker room being questioned, and I don't really remember who said what, but it turned into each one of us saying the other one did it—just a really dumb situation. Within a few days, Garrett and I finally matured and sat down together and talked. We decided we should have one another's back to stand up to the seniors. Not only that, but we were starting to become friends with all the same people. From that moment on, Garrett and I put aside our differences and became extremely close over the years.

We all would hang out and do crazy things together, from making our own personal "jackass" films, to our high school football games and practices where we would just laugh and talk smack to each other about how hard each one of us could hit the other, to joyriding in our parents' cars, to doing several other illegal things throughout our youth. We were wild kids, all of us. Our closest group was always myself, Garrett Kyle, Aaron Laub, Zach Nance, Brian Hanson, and Chris Anton. We five caused an insane amount of trouble and had so much fun doing it. Like I said, we were all wild children; we unleashed every ounce of courage and spontaneous energy we had on the small town of South Lake Tahoe. I will never regret a single thing I ever did with any of my close friends, especially Garrett.

Getting to know Garrett more and more and understanding him more showed me what a truly great person he was…he *is*. Yeah, sure, he had a "turbo" side, but he also had one of the biggest hearts of anyone. His laugh was unmistakable; it would always bring a warm smile to your face. Other great memories I shared with Garrett were hikes. We would walk and hike all over the place, go to the beach, to desolation wilderness. We would just look at a mountain and say, "let's climb that and see what the view is like."

Garrett eventually moved to Oregon with his family, and it did cause some separation from our group. Garrett and I would talk all the time when he first left. Then slowly more and more our connection between each other would fade more and more until eventually we barely ever talked. I remember he used to call me, and I would not even pick up anymore. In fact, the last time I ever spoke to him, he called me to talk and I said, "I don't have time to talk, and I'll have to call you back." He said "all right" and hung up. It still breaks my heart saying that or thinking about that moment, not knowing that would be the last time I would ever hear his voice or speak with him.

When I first heard about Garrett's passing, I was in shock. I was filled with so much anger and sadness. I was shaking and had started to sweat. When I heard the exact story of what happened, my first thought was, no way, there is no way that happened. I firmly believed someone did something to Garrett. I firmly believed Garrett wouldn't put himself in that situation. My head filled with horrible things I would do to the person who would hurt Garrett, how my friends and I would come to Oregon in search of ending someone else's life for taking our brother's life. Once I calmed down, I realized I need to not have anger, but instead hope and courage for Garrett, his family, and my other friends—for me to be strong for them, to give them strength. Nothing I could do, or can do, would bring Garrett back, not in his body anyways.

I feel Garrett almost every day through me. I feel him now as I am writing this. I feel him next to me; I see his face; I feel his embrace. I know he is always with me and looking out for me, and when my time comes, I know I will be reunited with him. I am so grateful for the friends and family of Garrett's I have met through this. Garrett's entire family is amazing and strong. I realized a big part of where Garrett's huge heart came from. It came from the people around him.

When I attended Garrett's memorial service, the amount of people there and the love felt in the room was incredible. I felt completely comfortable with everyone there, and I felt Garrett there. The entire time I was waiting for him to walk in, to say this isn't real, and he just wanted everyone he loved to be together in one room. But it never happened. It was real. It was as real as can be, and the sadness that ran through my heart and body that night I will never forget. It rained hard that day, like the sky was crying. I miss Garrett every day; I will always miss him, but I will never do anything but keep his memory alive and cherish the things he has taught me. Through him, I have met his wonderful mother Dana, his amazing father Kevin, his amazing stepfather Josh, his beautiful little brother Ryan, and his closest friends in Oregon, Lauren and Kelly. This group of people has made me into a better man, a better person in general.

I believe everything happens for reason, whether it is good or bad. Life will usually never go how it is planned, but that is the beauty of life. Not to get stressed or frustrated with life when it doesn't go your way, but to try and roll with it and understand it. Make life fun no matter what happens. Enjoy every single second, and make it count because you never know when your last day on this earth could be. To Garrett Michael Kyle, I know you can hear me, and know exactly what I am saying and feeling. I just want to say I love you with all of my heart, and thank you for being such an impact on my life and watching over me. Keep the sun shining for me and the ocean blue. I look forward to the next time I see you.

Love Always,

Jesse Chulay

Zach

I will always deeply miss and think about my closest friend/brother, Garrett Kyle. His passing changed me forever. I understand it is important to move on and continue living for one's own sake, but it does feel like part of me died when he did. After all we have been through together, we shared a very strong connection. He was the only young person I ever connected with spiritually in my young age, and I think that is a rare thing for young people. We were both smart beyond our years, and people told us so all the time. I believe we are indigo children through and through. Part of being an indigo child is having heightened spiritual awareness. This can be enlightenment and a burden at the same time. Extreme emotional and vibrational intellect can be very consuming. The world is a chaotic place with oceans of mixed energy. Sometimes we act in unexplainable ways, and I believe this is part of dealing with some of the intensity surrounding us.

Garrett in particular was a very special person. I think most people who knew him would agree with me. He always wanted everyone to have a good time. He was very loving and always made sure the feeling was mutual with his closest people. He would go to the extreme to make people laugh and deeply valued comedy and cinematography. Sometimes he or we would combine the two, and it always made for a good time and lots of laughs. He was always vibrant and just as comfortable in front of the camera as he was behind it. It was magical to watch and makes me wonder where he might have taken it if he had stuck around on this plane of existence.

I will never forget what Garrett did one bright and sunny summer day. It was my mom's AA birthday. At the time, this was sort of alien to me. I didn't really understand its importance or value its meaning to someone. Garrett and I were chilling at my house when my mom let us know that she would be leaving later that day. Garrett was always very inquisitive and had a goofy relationship with my mom, so he gathered the information that my mom would be going to her AA birthday. My mom always enjoyed Garrett's company and appreciated most of his humor. The conversation between him and my mom seemed to be getting a bit sarcastic with Garrett saying, "We will be showing up to attend your AA birthday" and my mom saying, "Oh gosh, you guys don't want to do that; go do something fun."

We went skateboarding for a while and, after a bit, Garrett said, "It's almost time for your mom's AA birthday. Dude, we better get going." I was a bit shocked; he was really serious about this, but I wasn't going to argue.

I could see he knew something about this that I did not. He was so serious that he stopped by Safeway and bought her flowers and a card! Then we were on our way.

The meeting had already started when we arrived. The room was full of people, and there was my mom and another person sitting at a table in the front of the room. Garrett gave me one of his signature looks and said, "They already started. Are you ready for this?" Without hesitation Garrett walked into the room with a giant bouquet of flowers in his arms, walked up to the table my mom was sitting at, set down the flowers, gave my mom a bear hug, grabbed a chair, and sat down next to her. My mom was really surprised. So surprised she started to cry. I was a little overtaken by all of this, but I followed his lead. The meeting continued on after that, and we sat next to her for the entire time. Later my mom took us out to dinner, and it was really a day for the books.

Ever since then, I always make it to my mom's AA birthday and bring her flowers just as Garrett had done for her that beautiful summer day years ago. My mom really cherishes that day and remembers Garrett by it especially. If I really put some effort to do so, I could probably write a book about the trials and tribulations of "Garrett and Friends." The times we all had together feel like yesterday and felt way too short. Garrett, I will always love you as my brother from another mother, and I miss you dearly. My only hope is that you could be there to greet me on the other side when my time comes.

Sincerely,

Zach Nance

As his friends shared their perspectives of Garrett, each one overwhelmed me to tears. Although our relationships were different, our perspectives and experiences with him were the same. It was more than confirmation or validation that others see Garrett as I do. It is a tribute to him, his light that touched so many with his love.

It's been years since his passing. A few of his friends and I still stay in contact. I have found this rather remarkable given they were teenagers when he transitioned.

After Garrett first passed, Halloween fell before we had Garrett's Celebration in November. It was a challenge to be festive. His friend Willie wanted to take Ryan trick or treating. He wanted to do it for Garrett and Ryan. Another friend, John, also wanted to go. They came over, and we carved pumpkins together. Both dressed up with Ryan and took him trick or treating and have made it an annual event. Ryan loves Halloween. Of course it's fun to dress up and get candy, but I know how much he looks forward to it every year—going with *his* friends, John and Willie.

Garrett's friend Joe shared this story after Garrett had passed. There was a homeless man in town known as the town drunk who rode this bicycle around town very slowly; he was known as "slowpoke." One day, Garrett and his friend were leaving his favorite burger place, and the man was out front. Garrett, curious as usual, started talking to the man, a man most people would and did walk by and ignore. Garrett asked him why he rode his bike so slow, and the man replied that he didn't have any brakes on his bike. Garrett reached into his pocket and gave the man twenty dollars. It was all the money Garrett had at the time.

Keeping the connection with Garrett's friends is a true gift. If Garrett were still in his body, I would have continued to see them as they would be in his life. In truth, as we are continuing on, Garrett is still very much with us. Most of us feel him. At first, I thought we were connected because of Garrett. What I have come to realize is that it is much bigger; we all are connected, although Garrett was the one who introduced us. They are more than just childhood friends of my son. They are like old friends, the ones you may not talk to for a long time, but when you get together it's as if there was no time in between. There's a special connection and understanding that's hard to describe. That's the feeling I have with these loving friends who have shared their hearts for this book and several others. On many occasions his friends will tell me that they feel Garrett with them, or they will call me and tell me they had the most wonderful vivid dream with him. It excites me that they share with me. It brings me so much joy to hear how Garrett is working his magic with so many people. I am enormously blessed by having these exceptional lights in my life.

Chapter Fourteen

Connecting with Garrett

Understanding shatters old
knowledge to make room for the
new that accords with reality.
—Thich Nhat Hanh

In the immediate weeks following Garrett's transition, I spent most of my time wondering what happened to him. Where was he? How was he? Why? Why did this happen? He was so happy, so connected, when he left. He had so much he wanted to do and share with others. Ryan just turned three when he passed, and I was heartbroken by my fear Ryan wouldn't be able to remember the brother who loved and adored him.

I kept processing all our last conversations, going back a week and reflecting on our conversation and then reflecting on conversations from two weeks ago: we were together and this happened. I kept cycling our most recent history. I was remembering everything we said to each other, everything that happened until he transitioned. I did this for about two years—remembering a year ago we did this, on this day, and two years ago this. When I shared this with a friend, he told me I had to quit doing this. It wasn't like that. I knew he was right, but I couldn't seem to help myself. It was as if the farther time went on, the farther Garrett would be away from me. I wanted to remember every bit of him, and these memories kept Garrett closer. Now when I think of times we spent together, when he was in his body, I do it from a place of love and feeling good—not from a place of feeling loss. It's a big difference. It's also not lost on me as I write this, it's the very time of year that I most reminisced. It feels good that I haven't been thinking the way I used to, and if I hadn't been writing, I would not have reminisced at all.

Before and during the time of Garrett's transition, I listened to online radio. A few months before Garrett passed, I began listening to Doreen Virtue, who is known for her work with angels, a subject I was interested in but knew little about. I enjoyed listening to the different shows before Garrett's passing. They felt like a lifeline afterward. That's when I began to listen to many well-known mediums as well. A medium is a title given to someone who can communicate with loved ones in nonphysical. This helped me tremendously, listening to those who were taking calls from people and connecting with their loved one in nonphysical, *on the spot*. It was healing to hear these messages, and I was learning about different signs our loved ones show us to let us know they are with us. Even though I had my own experiences with loved ones in nonphysical, I was raw, and I was struggling with what I knew in my heart, what I had been told, what most of the people I knew believed, and what our culture enforces. Listening to these shows helped to keep me grounded in my own knowing and inspired me to learn more. During this time, I heard Wayne Dyer talking about his experiences with two people who he loved that transitioned. It was helpful to know how he responded, and hearing his words of comfort reinforced my new thinking.

A few days before Garrett transitioned, I began reading a book that I had been tempted to read for months, but something about it made me uncomfortable. I wasn't quite sure about it. I began to hear some of the radio show hosts I was listening to talk about it and recommend it. I finally bought the book *Ask and It Is Given: Learning to Manifest Your Desires* by Esther and Jerry Hicks. It is a beautiful book that resonated deep within me, so much so that I didn't want to put it down. I read it every chance I got. It was this book I was reading the night the pain in my chest was so intense that I was wondering if I was going to have a heart attack. Over New Year's weekend, there was a marathon of Esther and Jerry Hicks workshops on the radio. I don't think I knew they did workshops or radio; I had *stumbled* upon it. That weekend I had the marathon playing and listened as much as I could. Their teachings reminded me of the Kabbalah teachings, unlike Kabbalah though in that it is not related to any religion. The workshops reflected the true spiritual connection that I wanted to better understand and know. Also, over that weekend, I finally began reading a book that had been sitting on my nightstand for months: *The Power of Now* by Eckhart Tolle.

After Garrett passed, I was not interested in books about grief. I was interested in reading spiritual books and books by mediums who connected with loved ones in nonphysical. That's what made me feel better. Focusing on where Garrett was, and that I could connect with him, was uplifting to me.

I was filling myself up with information that resonated with me at the deepest levels of my being. The old messages about death that I had been taught were not working for me. The best way to explain what was happening is similar to cleaning up a fragmented hard drive. I had so much information constantly going on in my mind that I finally had to clear and reboot it. That's exactly what I was doing—reprogramming myself, learning new ideas, challenging my beliefs, and downloading new information that I wanted to keep. It was information that made my heart sing. It's the light bulb coming on—*oh, so this is how it is!*—that makes so much sense.

Within a month of Garrett's passing, I tried getting an appointment with a medium and was turned down because this person felt it was too soon. The person wanted to wait three months before trying to connect with a loved one, so those in nonphysical have time to assimilate their transition. Three months seemed like an eternity. There was no way I could wait three months to talk to Garrett. At my worst, I was obsessed with these thoughts. I just wanted to know what happened to my boy. Where was my boy? I tormented myself with these types of thoughts.

A couple of opportunities did present themselves that gave me my answers. A coaching instructor of mine was also intuitive. I didn't know this until my coach told me about her. She was an angel and spent an hour with me sharing the visions and messages she received. One of the visions she shared was Garrett showing himself as a hawk, watching me.

Another connection was through a close friend of mine. Her hair stylist had also had a teenage son pass, and she was able to get the name of a medium from him for me. This appointment was also done over the phone, and it was a godsend. She was wonderful, and knowing Garrett was OK was healing beyond words could say. It was a huge relief.

Garrett first began to let me know he was around by running the water in the downstairs bathroom. This was happening fairly quickly after he passed. Within a few days of his passing, there was another sign from him. I keep a heavy crystal, wide-stemmed glass of water at my bedside table. I first noticed it askew on the coaster, which was strange. I wondered if it might be a sign from Garrett. Within a day or two of noticing the glass askew, I walked into my bedroom and saw the glass was on the carpeted floor broken. First, how did it fall? There had been no one in my room, and there was no way a glass like that would break from falling on the carpeted floor. I knew it was Garrett. Ryan's remote control car would start running when it was downstairs, even though the controller for it was upstairs and turned off. Things like this happened all the time for a few months.

Soon after Garrett passed, I began hearing a train. I had lived in my house a year and had never noticed hearing a train before. Now, at night, I was hearing a train all the time. His friends and his father began hearing trains, too. I heard the train for about two years. Now, five years later, although I live in the same house, I did not hear a train until I began writing this book, and I'm hearing the train again.

A couple of months after Garrett transitioned, a close friend of mine began dating an intuitive. On their first date, he asked her who the teenage boy was who was with her, and at first she didn't know. Then she remembered Garrett and told him her friend's son recently passed. He said, "He's here with you because he knows I can talk to him and can give a message to his mother." He was the first person to help me recognize my own clairvoyant abilities. He made me aware of the more subtle signs and ways to connect with Garrett and angels.

I learned I was seeing Garrett all the time and didn't realize it. This began very soon after Garrett transitioned. When I got into the car, I could see him changing the radio station. I didn't think much of it because it was something he always did when we got into the car together. I would see him at the mall. I could clearly see him walking toward me, wearing a big smile and his ball cap on backward. It was a few months before I found out that it really was Garrett. At the time I thought I saw him because I was thinking about him, wishing he was with me. I thought to see him that he would be an apparition in the room with me. Now I know all the times I saw him in my mind's eye, I was seeing him clairvoyantly (which I'll talk more about later). It was an everyday occurrence.

An incredible and joyful discovery was that Ryan was seeing him, too. Ryan would tell me Garrett was in the car with us. He would describe what he was wearing to me. He would talk to him all the time. At first I thought Ryan was talking to me. I would say, "What?" and he would say, "I'm talking to Garrett." I can't begin to tell you the joy, amazement, and relief I felt. Just a few weeks earlier I was crying because I feared Ryan would not remember his brother.

About six months after an appointment with the first medium, I connected with another one. During this session I was able to communicate with both my father and Garrett. Knowing they were together having a good time was another lift, another level of relief. During this visit, the medium told me that I was psychic, too. I shared that I had been told this before but never took it seriously. Of course I wanted to communicate and was excited anytime I did connect with Garrett. I couldn't get enough of him. After this appointment I began to be open to the idea of inviting more of this in.

CHAPTER FIFTEEN

Grief Group

For certain is death for the born, And certain is birth for the dead;
Therefore over the inevitable Thou shouldst not grieve.
—The Bhagavad Gita

I was coming full circle in a way I didn't want, another surreal experience. Ten years after I had been an intern and volunteer at The Dougy Center, I was now back as a participant with my three-year-old son. I was grateful for the resource. Ryan and I were lucky. We were able to get in a group quickly and began in November shortly after Garrett's celebration.

I found myself in a room filled with comfortable chairs, sofas, and broken hearts. When it was my turn to introduce myself, I could barely get the words out. They came with sobs and tears. "I'm Dana. I'm here because my nineteen-year-old son Garrett was hit by a train." Ryan was in the children's group, The Littles, which consisted of three- and four-year-olds. He was saying the same thing upstairs while cuddling a teddy bear.

The parent group is organized by the age of the child participating. Most parents in my group had experienced the passing of a young child. I'm the only one who had a teenager. I always felt a little different because Garrett was older, while my contemporaries were grieving babies and small children. This was completely self-inflicted. None of the wonderful facilitators or other parents ever made me feel awkward in any way. We were from different walks of life and every walk of life. It was a relief to be in a space where anything could be said, and no one judged anyone for his or her feelings. No one can know the depths of despair and unbearable pain of a child passing unless he or she experiences it. I kept thinking, *We are all in this club that nobody wants to be in.*

As the weeks and months progressed, no matter how I was feeling, it was still challenging for me to say that Garrett had been hit by a train and died. It surprised me that I would still get so choked up and emotional when I said these words. It became clear to me why it was difficult for me to say this. Although Garrett had been hit by a train, he did not die. It was not my belief system, so the words didn't fit my truth. Garrett was hit by a train, and although he had left his body, he did not die. Each time I said this in group, it wasn't my truth, and it was traumatizing to think of him as dead. But he wasn't dead; he just transitioned into a new form, one that I couldn't physically see but one I could very much clairvoyantly see and still feel. It was strange to be sitting in my group of peers of grieving parents and feel Garrett sitting next to me. Without a doubt he was with me.

I assumed there would be some parents who might be offended or fearful of my beliefs. I held back some of my experiences because I didn't want to offend anyone. As I thought more about it, I realized my beliefs and experiences, although they might be different from the mainstream, were just as valid. With this realization I put my fears of being judged aside and shared my experiences of feeling Garrett. The response amazed me.

Many of the other parents opened up about the similar experiences they were having. They also felt their children with them. There was one person in particular I was concerned about offending, but this was not the case at all. She contributed times when she felt her child, who was a bit closer in age to Garrett. It was as if the floodgates had opened up. I sensed it was a relief for all of us to share these experiences. Some shared of birds they just knew had something to do with their child, or flowers that had never bloomed before—all kinds of reassuring signs from their children. Some told how siblings were talking to the child who passed. I was glad that I had talked about my experiences with Garrett because it opened the door for others to speak about their experiences, which were not being expressed before my confession. I loved hearing these stories more than how we missed our child or what someone said that might have offended someone. It's strange that feeling connections with our children turned out to be a common occurrence; yet, we parents were reluctant to talk about what seemed to be universal connections. Why are we so guarded about this? I was afraid of what the others would think of me. Come to find out, they were having similar experiences.

Over time we had many sessions where we talked about dreams and signs that we knew were from our children. Some could even hear their children. We were grieving our children's passings and talking about all the ways they were trying to communicate with us, letting us know they are still near us. How ironic.

There is one thing I noticed within myself and observed in others: there seems to be in this society a sense that the amount of pain, grief, and suffering that we put ourselves through represents how much we love the person who has passed. It's as if it's a badge of love for the person who passed. If I suffer this much because you're gone, you and everyone else will know how much I love you. It doesn't need to be this way at all. Of course there are the emotions of grief that are important to process, but allowing grief to linger serves no one.

Fairly soon after Garrett's passing, I noticed Ryan was seeing and talking to Garrett. I wondered if it was confusing for him to be saying his brother died. I know in the groups, it's the same with the children as with the adults. They say who and how their loved one died. If children continue to see and speak to their loved one, it must get confusing. I believe we have an innate knowing that we don't die and this knowing is taught out of us. Therefore, grieving is a state of mind that is taught to us.

Ryan didn't cry when we told him Garrett was hit by a train. I know that developmentally children can't comprehend death until about the age of nine, I think it is important to look at what really *happens* to a child's belief system. I believe that *they* are saying that it is at this age that children see death the same way most adults in their life now see death. This is about the age that children also begin to lose that innocence and their connection to their own knowing. In essence, this is the age that children begin to trust the adults around them more than their own knowing. We are taught that our loved ones are gone, that we lose connection with them, and that passing is unnatural. Children go against their own knowing based on what they are told by adults.

After about four months, I began to notice that I was feeling different. I wasn't in the same space as when I first began the group, and I began to notice that the energy started to bring me down. While I had compassion for everyone and our experiences, I was getting the sense this was no longer the best place for me. I began to feel as if I was absorbing some of the energy from others in the room. While I loved and respected our group, I felt it was time for me to move on. Completing the group is left up to the child, not the parent. I was ready. I had been ready for a while, but Ryan still wanted to attend. Frankly, I didn't think he would want to stop going; there were so many wonderful activities for him, and he loved it. After about seven months, Ryan told me he was done. I love how children just know, and it was no big deal that he was done. He knew why he was there, and then he was complete with his process.

During my time in our groups, I was asking for wisdom, praying *please give me wisdom to understand this situation.* Sometimes I felt a certain knowing and would share. The day I said good-bye to my group, there was a tug in my heart. I was ready to move on and had a desire to stay and help. People shared that they appreciated the wisdom in what I had shared, that I had helped them. This acknowledgment touched me deeply. My learning had not only helped me; it had also helped the other parents. Grieving a child is tapping into the depths of one's own heart. Sharing it with other grieving parents provides a deep heartfelt connection.

These groups are based on anonymity. We don't share other people's stories. In honor of this, I didn't go into details. I will share, however, that I saw some profound changes in parents' lives that, to me, were clearly a direct result of their child's passing. It's as if the children in their passing leave the gift of helping their parent, or parents take their life to a higher purpose. I know this is my story, and I am in good company.

Our dog Chico, at ten years old, became sick five months after Garrett's transition. I thought she was going to pass, too, but miraculously she pulled out of it. A month later, it was Garrett's dog, BJ, who unexpectedly passed at the age of eleven, six months after Garrett. Ryan saw BJ's body after he had left it and was curious that he wasn't moving. I shared with him that he had left his body, hopefully to help him understand. At first, I didn't think he really understood because he kept talking about BJ as if he were still around. Later it finally dawned on me that he was most likely seeing and maybe feeling BJ around as well.

My experience with BJ's passing was beautiful. He became sick over the weekend, and I was going to take him to the veterinarian first thing Monday morning. He was too sick to make it upstairs and too large for me to carry, so I slept on the couch that night to be near him. I woke up at about four in the morning and checked on him and discovered he had transitioned. My heart was sad yet relieved for him. He was too big for me to move, so I went upstairs to my room and lay down on my bed. I woke up about an hour later and looked down at the floor next to my bed where he normally slept, and I could see him there. For a moment I thought I dreamed he had passed, until I looked again and did not see him.

My reaction to his passing was different from what it would have been if I hadn't been going through the transformation with Garrett's transition. I would have been devastated. Of course nothing compares to a child passing, but it was more than that. I had changed my thinking. I did have the thought, *One more extension of Garrett, the dog he loved now gone, too.* It wasn't pleasant, but I was much less resistant about his passing. Three months later, Chico passed, It was tough. I wasn't expecting either of the dogs to pass. They *seemed to be* too young to pass, just like my thoughts of Garrett in the beginning of my grief. Our dogs are members of the family. The gift in the timing was that I was in a place of accepting that they were ready to leave, and it was OK.

After the passing of both BJ and Chico, my friend's son came over to play with Ryan. This little boy was about six at the time. I was in my office, and he came in and asked me, "Where is the black dog?" I told him there isn't a black dog here. He said he saw him by the stairs and then, very matter of fact, told me that he sees things that other people don't and went back to playing.

I, too, often see BJ and Chico around the house or with us when we go on walks. They pop in. The year that they passed I often felt them lying in my office, which is where they always were before they transitioned. It was comforting to feel their presence and know that they were around me.

Chapter Sixteen

Court

The truth is more important
than the facts.
—Frank Lloyd Wright

I resumed my coaching practice about four months after Garrett passed. My professional life began going well. I began developing and teaching coaching and leadership development classes at Marylhurst University, which was a dream of mine. I also contracted with a career development company to coach their clients. My commitment to Garrett's Space was important, and I was in the beginning phase of building a board.

About two and a half months after Garrett passed, another concern for Ryan's safety—while with his father—had surfaced. This situation made my life stressful beyond anything I could ever have imagined. This compounded the intensity of my grief and, at times, was a distraction from it. Just when I thought I couldn't feel any more victimized, Josh and I spent the time following our divorce with lawyers in disagreement over Ryan's well-being. We had just come to an agreement regarding Ryan before Garrett's passing. Now the same issues were popping up again, only this time with a meth addict. What was to ensue became the most stressful legal battle I had ever experienced. It was as ugly as it gets. To say that I was livid would be an understatement. This became the most emotional and financially stressful time of my life.

I have never been angry with Garrett for transitioning. But I was furious that I had to grieve my son's passing and, at the same time, deal with the high stress of family court. I was going on year three in family law, and it was grueling. This situation would have been stressful at any time, but given Garrett's recent transition, I was in a whole new arena. It was a heavy weight to bear.

I couldn't get past my anger and resentment at Ryan's dad for being irresponsible and out of control with his life. I was angry that he couldn't behave within the law and honor our agreements, and that I felt I needed to give my time and energy to this, when I only wanted to grieve Garrett and take care of Ryan. I was mad at God for putting me in this situation. I was angry about the feeling of a never-ending battle with Josh. For two and a half years, he'd been this thorn in my side. It seemed that all I was learning was not being applied in this situation. I seemed to be stuck repeating the same circumstances, which frustrated me to no end. I couldn't figure out how to make it stop. Choosing peace in this situation seemed impossible; accepting the situation seemed irresponsible. Emotions from the past two and half years and the grieving seemed to play out here.

If the situation had been about anything but Ryan's safety and well-being, I would have let it go. What I cared deeply about was my baby son whose safety and well-being were paramount. I was in mama-bear mode and not about to back down. I realize these feelings were from a place of feeling like a victim, and I'm sharing it like it was, how I was feeling at the time. I have changed significantly since this happened and now can see the blessings from my antagonist.

In the following chapters, I will tell you how I was able to emerge from this chaos with not only my sanity but also my peace of mind, a healed relationship and, eventually, appreciation for all of it.

My beautiful blond-haired, blue-eyed boy Garrett on his fifth birthday. It was all about ninja turtles back then.

Garrett and me happy to be in Lake Tahoe 1996.

Garrett with his beloved dog BJ.

Garrett and me after his wedding toast.

Taking time for a pose.

Feeling like king of the mountain.

Proud big brother.

Ryan showing Garrett how it's done on the court.

The smile that lights up the room.

So happy celebrating Ryan's third birthday,
one month before Garrett's transition.

Chapter Seventeen

Spiritual Awakening

In the midst of winter, I finally learned
there was in me an invincible summer.
—Thomas Carlyle

I learned from Garrett's passing that when someone close passes, everyone is given the opportunity for a spiritual awakening, the desire to understand what happened and why. Where was my son? I wanted to know. For a while these questions were all I could think about. The desire was strong, and I know that is how I was able to discover the answers I was asking for.

When you're shaken to your core, you can live in pain, bitterness, resentment, guilt, and feelings of victimization. Or, you can look for the peace that makes you stronger; you can go within and discover what's really there.

When nothing makes sense, the information you have doesn't feel right, it's time to begin to look at life from a spiritual perspective rather than a physical perspective. It is from the spiritual perspective you'll receive your answers and find peace.

When Garrett transitioned I began to let go of the small, irritating things in my life; they just didn't matter. I was just trying to figure out how I could stop feeling the unbearable pain I was experiencing. It took a while for me to get back on track, to do mundane things like pay my bills. I didn't care as much what others might think. What I did care about was feeling better and wanting to know where my son was. I wanted to talk to him and understand what had happened.

All I wanted to do was talk about Garrett; everything reminded me of him. I wanted to know that he was OK, to know where he was. At first, I wanted to know exactly what had happened. When I began hearing some details, I realized I didn't want to know because it didn't matter. Nothing was going to change the outcome, and the sooner I got past it, the quicker I would feel peace.

It's important to know we stay connected with each other, whether in the physical or nonphysical. There is very little difference. The Consciousness of our loved ones is still very much available to us in the physical at any time. We are eternal. Nothing goes wrong. We are always safe. It's from our physical perspective there is judgment that things go wrong. Leaving our bodies is not a bad thing. There is nothing to fear because it's not the end—only a rebirth, a continuation of our eternal journey.

What I've learned as a result of Garrett's transition is that most of what I was taught about death is not true. There is no death as most of us have been taught. Rather, your Consciousness (Soul) leaves your body and raises to a higher vibration into a nonphysical dimension. You leave only your body behind. Consider your body a house for your Soul. It is the vehicle you use to interact while you are in this physical Earth plane. Your Consciousness is omnipresent, like angels and God. This Consciousness can participate in the Earth's dimension and others. This is what I've come to know to be true. I know it. My entire being knows this truth. I have experienced interactions with many a Consciousness in nonphysical.

External circumstances do not provide peace. Circumstances are put before us to help us understand who we are, to come to know we are spiritual beings. Realize your loved one who passed has given you a great gift, to have the opportunity to come to know this truth.

I realized my grief was not only about wanting to see and connect with Garrett in his physical body. That was clearly over. My grief came from thinking/believing that I would never have contact with him again, or at least until I, too, passed. My pattern of thought was so ingrained. Even though I had connected with my grandfather and father in non-physical, it had been forgotten. I came to know that I had been given the opportunity to know and love Garrett from a new perspective, that our communication would continue, and, that our relationship would grow—forever. Having this knowing helped tremendously while I assimilated his passing and began to reconcile my beliefs and align them with my own knowing. It was a process that didn't happen overnight. I had old patterns to change, and I flip-flopped many times.

I wasn't always sure that I was really connecting to Garrett. Even though I had the powerful experience in the funeral home, there were times I still doubted my ability. My "old belief" that talking with those in nonphysical was for the psychics and mediums—not everyday people like me, continued to surface at times.

My huge realization during this time was that we are all intuitive; we all have these capabilities. It's not just for those who are labeled *psychic* or *medium*. Somehow people who have developed this skill became labeled abnormal, different. The truth is, we all have this. It's what most of us call our gut feeling or instincts. Another word that describes these is *intuitive*. When we hone and trust these senses, just like any other skill, we get better at them.

I no longer view someone transitioning as a tragedy or untimely. My beliefs, as they are not mainstream yet, have made it a bit awkward when I'm around others who have traditional cultural fears about passing. However, this is shifting. Having the experience of a son pass, sharing my grief process and my personal transformation of cultural beliefs about death is a gift from Garrett.

Connecting with Garrett helped me to embrace my intuitive knowing and awaken to another level of depth that we are eternal; relationships are eternal; and there is only a perception of division between the physical and nonphysical. There is no veil. Our loved ones in the nonphysical are present to all of us.

Now when someone passes, it feels bittersweet at first, for a little bit. It's a practiced first response. Once I remind myself of the truth and send love to those who have transitioned and their loved ones, I feel better. I change my focus to the love that I have for the person, or furry friend, and know that we can still communicate; our relationship is far from over.

Grieving reminds me of a quote by Byron Katie, *Suffering is optional*. While I understand and have at times missed my son in his body, I can communicate with him. Once you can get to a place of surrender and love, you will understand what I am saying. It is a completely different way of thinking and being than I was taught. It reminds me of the time Garrett left home. While I was happy for my son, seeing him grown up was bittersweet. My little boy was all grown up. Thinking of your transitioned loved one in this similar manner might help you. It really is no different; our loved ones have grown and moved on, but you can still have a relationship with them. It will be different only in that they aren't in their body, and they will have a broader view.

I hope this helps you as you move through your grief process. I used to fear transitioning, and my greatest fear of all was that I would have a child pass before me. I was much like everyone else in my beliefs about passing. Know the opportunity to face a fear is a great blessing.

CHAPTER EIGHTEEN

Beliefs

It is your own assent to yourself, and the constant voice of your own reason, and not of others, that should make you believe.
—Blaise Pascal

My work, both personal and professional, has taught me to be aware of my beliefs, that they create our reality. How we live is based on our beliefs. Beliefs are thoughts that we think continuously until we believe them. We might have a belief that something can't be done, and then one person does it, and it changes the belief. Our beliefs create what we live.

Beliefs can empower or disempower. My beliefs about death at the time my son passed were disempowering and limiting. Next, I began to *sort out* my belief systems—the old practiced beliefs competing with my intuitive knowing. Out of my personal experiences and teachings in spirituality, which validated my experiences, came my new beliefs. My new beliefs on death changed so radically that I no longer use this word.

Intuitively, I've known for a long time that our beliefs limit us. When I was about thirty, working for a large corporation and going to school to get my college degree, I was evaluating how I wanted to move forward with my life. I could feel something inside me wanting a change. During that time, I was running every day. I enjoyed it because running cleared my mind. I didn't know then that running can be a form of meditation. One day while I was running, I realized that I could do anything I wanted. There was no one holding me back. I could so clearly see that we create our own prisons by the way we think. Until this point, I only saw one path for my life and that was the corporate world. In this moment I saw a new landscape open up. It was exhilarating.

My new awareness helped me tremendously during my grief process. I noticed when things that others said, or that even I said, felt *off.* I continued to go with them because these were thoughts I had grown up believing. They were beliefs I had never before questioned. After Garrett passed, I began to question everything. (I'm going to use the words *death* and *dead* here because when I was in this space, I was using these words.)

I questioned death. I questioned all my beliefs about death. What happens when we die? Where do we go? Can we really communicate with the dead? Even though I had experiences with my father and grandfather, I still questioned God, spirituality, what's really important. I wanted to hear what mediums and spiritual teachers had to say about death and talking to loved ones who had died. Through these and very personal experiences, I changed many beliefs.

It changed the way I grieved, and I challenged myself. When I found myself thinking painful thoughts about Garrett, I began reminding myself what I believed. If I really believe he's with me, why am I choosing this thought instead of what I am experiencing and what I know to be true? It was the process of breaking down old patterns and old beliefs that, to some degree, were never really mine. But I thought them and, therefore, believed them. I became vigilant in my self-awareness. I wanted to feel better. I wanted peace and wanted to feel joy in my heart again, which seemed like an impossible task in the beginning. I began to take control of myself. It was a process and a discipline.

There were many unwanted things going on in my life during the first year of Garrett's passing that I could not control. This I could control, so it was important to me. I listened to teachings that talked about the nonphysical, and I began to literally reprogram myself. I was filled with beliefs and habits of thought my entire life that no longer worked for me. I was changing and consciously living my spiritual beliefs like I never had before. I *had* to walk the talk. I was given an opportunity to share something quite profound and life-changing.

I didn't want Ryan to forget Garrett. Even though that thought broke my heart, it didn't stop me from thinking the thought, having the belief. Later when I realized that Ryan had been in touch with Garrett all along, I was overjoyed. Ryan is eight years old and in daily communication with Garrett, and I know he always will be. He just told me yesterday that Garrett is his best friend. It's interesting, really. I felt so raw thinking of

Ryan not knowing Garrett. I tormented myself with this belief. Today it is a nonissue. I can see how needless my pain was over this thought. It did not serve me. It wasted my energy and proved to be false.

During this time of change and challenging my beliefs, I began to feel judgment from some of my close friends. I felt judgment about the choices I was making in my career; I felt judgment about my beliefs; and I also noticed that I began to judge them judging me. I didn't like this. What became clear, and if I am to be honest, a shift had been a long time coming. Even before Garrett passed, I began feeling a disconnect. It happens, and that's why many people stay put. They are afraid of not being accepted. When you change, everyone may not come with you. Ryan's father was my biggest disappointment. He made it clear he wasn't coming with me. I couldn't imagine going forward without a couple of dear lifelong friends, but that is what had to happen. I had been dishonoring my beliefs to fit in. After Garrett's passing, I wasn't willing to do this anymore. I realized it was OK to let go. It doesn't mean I love them any less; it's that I'm choosing to move forward in a new way, a way that honors who I am. While this was happening, doors to new, like-minded friends opened up.

It may not be easy to let go of friendships, but there are times when it's a natural part of your own evolution. The tribe doesn't like it when someone bucks the system. It makes them uncomfortable. As you make changes, it can make others uncomfortable. You are rocking the status quo. That's OK; to each his own. I found I was no longer willing to hold back who I am in my process of discovering. It serves no one to stay small.

Chapter Nineteen

Love or Fear

Love seeketh not itself to please, Nor for itself hath any care, But for another gives its ease, And builds a Heaven in Hell's despair.
—William Blake

We have two choices. We can respond from either a place of love or a place of fear. What I mean by a place of love or fear is the perspective from which you're viewing the situation. In any given moment, what is prompting your emotions? Our natural way of being is grounded in love, which is complete congruency. When grounded in love, you have feelings of peace, happiness, and joy. You have the feeling of eternalness, connection, and a sense that everything is going to be all right, even if you don't know how circumstances will come about.

Everything else is fear based; this is where death resides. Fear is the thinking that something has gone or will go terribly wrong. Fear is worry, doubt, not forgiving, guilt, and stress. It's all the emotions tied in with grief, anger, heartbreak, guilt, and so forth. In all my legal interactions, I was coming from a place of fear.

Whether you come from a place of love or fear is always your choice.

Our Western culture is grounded in fear, and fear of death is the biggest fear we have. There seems to be a pervading belief that passing is the most unnatural and terrible thing in the world that can happen.

I grew up in the Christian faith believing that when you die, you go to heaven and meet up with God and your loved ones who have already passed. In heaven you will see everyone else again when they "die" too, but in the meantime they are out of your life. There are the unfortunate ones who are judged, or who don't embrace Jesus for whatever reason, and they go to hell, an unpleasant place from the images I've heard and seen depicted in books and movies.

My greatest fear was that none of this was true, and that we die and there is nothing. That there would be nothing was my darkest thought. Moreover, those of us who experienced the passing of a loved one were left with the unspeakable pain of enduring life without that loved one. We'd long for our loved one, grieve, and feel that emptiness inside until we, too, passed and reconnected.

When you look at death as most do in our culture, it is based completely on fear. Rarely is it embraced. We tend to keep people and pets going through test after test and surgery after surgery with no quality of life because of this fear. It's understandable when coming from a fear-based place why death is to be avoided at all costs. Most of us think tragedies, such as children dying before their parents, are wrong. This is an arrogant assumption. It's like saying our Creator has made a huge mistake. We fear the unknown, and in the known we find fear on most subjects in our lives. This is the message that Garrett was sharing with me when he had the mystical experience. He saw how we fear so many things we are not present to but drive us.

Coming from fear, it is understandable why death is unwanted. We don't want the people we love to leave their life. I felt this way. I couldn't imagine anything worse than having my son die. I specifically had this fear for about a year when he was nine-years-old. When Garrett was in high school, he had several classmates transition, and he was crushed by their passing. I had compassion for the kids, but my heart broke for the children's parents having to endure the pain of losing a child. I didn't know then what I have since learned—that no one is lost.

When you come from a place of love, which is from a spiritual perspective, you're congruent with your higher self. You can see the blessings that each person's life brings to you. You know that nothing has gone wrong, and there were great gifts given to you by your loved ones. If you cannot see them in the moment, you know they will be revealed to you. This is true not just for a loved one passing but for any unwanted situation in which you may find yourself.

When you are grounded in love, there is an opportunity for each of us to have a spiritual awakening. This is what happened to me.

It's easy to come from a place of love when holding a baby or a new puppy or kitten, when things are going right in your life. It's a spiritual challenge to be grounded in love when things aren't going as you planned. I've learned it's the reason we have unwanted things in our life—so that we can come to know the true love that exists within each of us. Most of us can't seem to do that unless there is some adversity to overcome, and even then it's not a given. It's always a choice: How do I want to be? You make the choice whether you are conscious of it or not.

When I was at the five-year anniversary of September 11, it was just a month before Garrett passed. Hearing the grief in the family members' voices, I knew that so many were nowhere near peace. Little did I know, a month later my son would transition, and I would have a similar shock. Remembering these families helped me to move forward. I knew that I wanted to be in a different place five years after Garrett's passing.

I am a lot like Garrett in that we both are passionate about wanting others to know what we know. It was important for him to let others know that we all have a path, that there are things that are Divinely planned. We are all connected, and love is the key to all our problems.

There is a Creator, an energy, Consciousness, God, the Divine, whatever you want to call it, that is pure love and omnipresent. We are all part of this eternal Consciousness. This love is perfect. It is our skewed perspective, our fear-based thoughts, that trip us up. Once you know that your transition to your body and the transition from your body are Divinely planned, there really is nothing to fear. You are safe. Then, you can relax, enjoy your life, and connect with your loved ones who are waiting for you to do so.

When being consoled, what I've found is that sympathy does not feel better. What does feel better is genuine compassion. When someone is sympathetic, he or she comes from a place of fear—something like, "Oh, I'm so sorry; this is terrible." Notice the undercurrent of "I feel so sorry for you." I guess the rebel in me doesn't like anyone feeling sorry for me or Garrett, or anyone else. It feels wrong. It can make someone feel worse than he or she already feels. I've been in situations where I'm feeling OK about Garrett passing, and someone tries to share his or her sympathy with me. I feel it's more about that person than about where I'm at.

Coming from a place of compassion is a completely different energy. The best I can describe it is a place of love. The person does not judge but instead feels love for all concerned. There is a connection of understanding, of the pain someone might be feeling, but minus the sense of pity. I remember and can clearly feel the feeling I had when a close friend was coming from a place of compassion. We were talking on the phone not long after Garrett had passed, and she was checking in on me. We had this beautiful moment when we cried together. I could feel her love and her genuine presence with me. She wasn't feeling sorry for us; she was just being with me. Compassion is all about love, and you have an opportunity to help someone focus on his or her truth. Being compassionate is being in love—or you can reaffirm and influence fears.

When Garrett passed, I vacillated many times between love and fear. I was certainly coming from a place of fear with the court case. I knew it. As I tried to get my spiritual footing, I was overwhelmed with so many fears for Ryan's well-being and all that surrounded it. At the time, I did the best I could.

When I embraced Garrett's passing, I was able to let go of my grief, my fear, and come from a place of love. This is what transformed within me. The hole in my heart felt like the size of the Grand Canyon. Reflecting back, it's like a miracle to have transformed those feelings to the peace and sometimes overwhelming love I feel today.

CHAPTER TWENTY

Surrender

Nothing can bring you peace but yourself.
—Ralph Waldo Emerson

Garrett transformed back into the nonphysical and embraced it much better than I embraced my opportunity to transform. It did happen. I did allow the grace of the Divine to fill and heal my heart—to the point that on the three-year anniversary of his passing, I felt sheer joy and connection with my beautiful son, feelings it took three years to get back. It all happened with my desire for peace, joy, and connection with my son, which I achieved with many angels on earth and in nonphysical.

If you have a desire to experience this as well, please know it can be done. I'm proof. I've learned our connections are never severed, and our love for our loved ones who've passed can grow stronger, just as if they were still in their bodies.

Surrender is the most important piece to well-being. Without it, it's impossible to find peace. Surrender may sound like a weakness as it means to cease resistance—which means to give up. It also means to abandon oneself entirely to a situation. To know peace is to give up resistance; it is to fully surrender to what is.

This means accepting what has happened to your loved one and fully accepting how you are feeling. Acceptance means this is what happened; this is where I am, and I have no judgment about any of it. It just is.

After all the dwelling on whys, what-ifs, and if-onlys, after all these painful, disempowering, and useless thoughts, I was left feeling no better, usually worse. How could I even begin to feel even a little bit better now that my beloved son has left his body? Nothing will be the same; that is for sure; everything has changed. These thoughts brought me to a frightening finality. There is no going back, and being where I was, my now was unbearable. What's left? What were my options?

When I found myself in this place, I remember saying to a close friend of mine, "If only I had worried about him." She wisely responded, "Do you really think you have that much power?" That moment I realized how ridiculous my thought was. Her words immediately reminded me this was the making of something far greater than I could even begin to comprehend. How egotistical of me to think that I could change the Divine wisdom involved.

We have to make a choice: the choice to stay an emotional wreck or the choice to find grace in a situation.

The step was to surrender. I had to surrender to what is. As long as I was stuck in the what-ifs and whys, I was resisting the reality of the situation and keeping myself from the relief I so badly wanted. That's what made me feel so miserable—resisting what is and not accepting.

I decided that I wanted to be a fully present and loving mother to Ryan. I knew I would find a gift if I did the work. I didn't want it at first, but I eventually surrendered to all of it, even to the situation with Ryan's father. I had to quit resisting that situation and come from an entirely new place if I was to feel peace.

I expended too much energy in my resistance. No wonder I felt so powerless and spent many days with inner turmoil. Being able to surrender is acceptance; it is the chance to embrace something new. There is only power in acceptance, which allows you to move forward.

After Garrett transitioned, I didn't have any peace until I surrendered. I decided to quit cycling on the details, especially the fact that he was no longer in his body. So, I began to embrace and surrender to the situation. Once I did this and began to focus on our new relationship, I had peace and have discovered many blessings and the grace that comes with what I know to be a gift—his leaving his body. This was not easy. I started the process feeling the most unbearable emotional pain imaginable. I practiced over and over, reminding myself I wanted to feel better. It didn't happen overnight. I had to work at it.

I chose to change my thoughts. I stopped thinking that something was wrong and rather, began to look for the gifts in what is. And, every time I make that choice, I allow Garrett to be with me in an even more profound way. I began to embrace the unwanted, which eliminated the fear. I also let go of self-judgment, which was huge to my peace of mind. It's not the situation that defines you; it's how you move through it. This is what I remind myself of when I encounter a challenge. How do I want to move through this one?

Surrendering is making a choice that you are ready to let go of your pain. Usually, you are in so much pain that you just can't continue the way things have been going. This point is different for each person and situation. It could be days, weeks, months, years. At some point, you decide you are no longer willing to feel bad. You become tired of the energy it takes to resist. When you resist, you stay in a place of powerlessness. Isn't that what's happening when a loved one passes? You feel powerless; your heart is broken, and it is unbearable at times.

Once you let go of your resistance to what is, you begin to open the door to a peaceful heart ,which allows grace into the situation. This prompts a shift in your perspective. You can begin to see the grace in all situations. You'll see there are no accidents or mistakes, that everything is Divinely happening in its own perfect way, even if the situation makes no sense from your perspective. Surrender is the releasing of your resistant energy emotions of anger, guilt, and regret. The serenity prayer is a prayer of surrender:

God, grant me the serenity to accept the things I cannot change;
courage to changethe things I can; and the wisdom to know the difference.
— Reinhold Niebuhr

What helped me to surrender was my spiritual connection and beliefs. I knew deep in my heart that Garrett was supposed to leave his body, even though it felt to me far too early. A part of me knew this was not a mistake or an accident but something much bigger.

It took time for me to get my head and heart congruent, and when I did, I was able to accept that this was all right, that nothing had gone wrong. This gave me an incredible amount of peace and clarity about Garrett's transition. It was a process.

Surrender is letting go of judgment. In our society, how people pass, their age when they pass, has a tremendous amount of judgment, which, for those who are grieving, only intensifies the pain. There are many negative judgments concerning transitioning. These judgments make it even more difficult to heal because we end up believing them, too. Michael Jackson and Whitney Houston are good examples. When they passed, every report I heard, spoke of their "untimely" deaths, the what-might-have-beens, all the drama about the wrongness of it all. These are not the words or thoughts that support healing. At one time I would have agreed with those sentiments. These are arrogant statements. Who says it's untimely? Who is making that judgment? So many agree with these sentiments, but they are fear-based statements. I know it was the perfect time for them to transition. There was nothing untimely about it. There is no law that says everyone leaves at an old age. Somehow, if people leave before whatever age is deemed appropriate, then it's wrong. There are so many judgments, beliefs, and opinions thrown around that we all just seem to go along with them. We don't question them, even when they feel off.

When celebrities pass, their loved ones often say during interviews that they feel them or hear them, but this is completely overlooked. No one digs deeper. It makes me wonder if the interviewer even heard what was said.

Those who commit suicide are judged. There is guilt and shame for the family members of those who choose this means of exit. But we are not to judge one another; we do not know. These are decisions made on a Soul level, and we do not know the paths of other Souls. We can love the person, honor our grief process, and know that our loved one is held with love. People are not punished for the way they leave their bodies.

Surrender does not mean that you—in any way—love your loved one less. There is no gold star for suffering.

When you surrender, you allow love into your heart, love for yourself. This is when you think of your loved ones. You can feel them, and you can lovingly reflect on the gifts they brought and will bring to your life.

My mother had a very difficult time surrendering. It took her a few years. She shared with me what turned things around for her. Rather than focusing on Garrett not being here, she decided to appreciate the time she had with her grandson, the nineteen years of his life, and how much joy he brought to her. That's what made the difference in alleviating her grief.

I don't know of a more challenging situation to surrender to than the passing of a loved one, but when you can get to this place, it's an opportunity for spiritual awakening that changes everything in your life.

I was so angry over the constant issues with my ex-husband. I thought once the house sold and the divorce was complete, that would be the end of my stress, but it seemed to be the beginning. It was nonstop for almost three years. Coupled with Garrett's transition, I was feeling extremely angry and frustrated. A couple of months after our final court date, I reflected on what had happened. I had been focused on the dishonesty. It was beyond me. I was reviewing the courtroom scene in my mind—the ridiculousness of it—and stepping back and reflecting. It was almost a dark comedy.

During the legal drama, I just wanted peace. I had written an affirmation that I had kept in my office and said it several times every day. My affirmation was, "I have peace and harmony in all my relationships." At this point peace was paramount. I was surrendering and embracing Garrett's transition better than I was dealing with the antagonist in my life. As I was reflecting on the courtroom drama, I could see and feel the anger from my ex-husband on the witness stand, and I realized in that moment two things.

First, this situation wasn't me. It was not who I was in any way, and that is one reason why I felt so bad. I had allowed myself to be sucked into a drama that was not me. I had never had so much unrest in my life before this experience. Very few people knew the extent of the circumstances. I didn't share a lot with my family because I didn't want to upset them and make it into something bigger.

My second realization was a huge revelation. I was really angry with myself for not being true to myself and for giving someone else so much power over me. I had justified it as the safety and well-being of my young son. I feel I took the appropriate steps any parent would take in the situation. During this process, I was incongruent, grounded in fear. This was causing my anger, my feeling of powerlessness. I had to *be* my affirmation—not just *say* it but begin to *be* it.

While reflecting and seeing myself in this light, I decided to be me no matter what anyone else did. Even with my concerns about safety unresolved, I decided this wasn't going to deter me.

I also decided to let go of the need to be right. If I wanted to be me, I had to let go of it, no matter how inflammatory I felt things were. I had to surrender to the situation and accept where things stood. To have the peace that I desired, I had to quit playing a role that wasn't mine.

I did surrender, and the result is a completely transformed relationship. It took a while, as did practicing my new beliefs. I made it a priority for myself to feel peace and be the loving person I am. I let go of the anger;

there was no need to hold on to it because it wasn't me. What I've come to know about myself is that any time I find myself angry, it's because I have moved out of alignment with who I am.

This was all part of my surrender, to let go of another piece in my life that I was resisting. People who saw what I experienced and have witnessed the transformation view it as a miracle. And it is—one that I allowed to happen.

Now, I can simply appreciate it all and can laugh about much of it. Even though I had a fantastic antagonist, I know none of my pain was really about him. It was about me giving up my power and not being true to myself. It's so clear to me now. I would not know this without the experience. To accept, to surrender to what is, no matter how stressful—and, as a parent, there is nothing more stressful than worrying over the well-being and safety of your children. To be who you are and true to yourself is to access your power and have peace within. When you find peace, you've found grace and an appreciation for the entire experience. This is forgiveness. It's internal; it's personal; and it has nothing to do with anyone else, what they've done or said. It's only about you.

Chapter Twenty-One

It's Only Change

What then is the true gospel of consistency? Change.
—Mark Twain

The passing of a loved one is change, a big change, and I invite you to try to begin to look at change in the way that supported me. Yes, there is definitely a physical change. My son was no longer in his body; that was a major unwanted change in my life. After some time, I realized my internal change was just as big as his leaving his body felt. We both were evolving, Garrett back into the nonphysical and me spiritually. We were both growing, and are still growing together, just as we had been growing when Garrett was in his body. The realization of this perspective was liberating and exciting.

My life experiences have provided an abundance of change, plenty of unwanted and wanted. Most people, no matter what change they are experiencing, tend to resist it. Most tend to fear any unknown, even if they know they will ultimately feel better. It's been my job to help people shift perspectives and move through change with grace—not to fear change but to learn to embrace change and embrace the growth opportunity that change provides. In the weeks following Garrett's transition, I didn't appreciate the opportunity to embrace this change. Garrett's passing took embracing change to an entirely new level.

All change has the potential to lift you to a new, wonderful place of Being. I felt I was being tested to see if what I thought I believed about death was true. How could I ease this transition? This was difficult, uncharted territory. There is no skipping around things; we all have to do our work. There is no silver bullet that is going to resolve internal turmoil. This type of turmoil doesn't go away. You can try to ignore it or medicate it, but at the end of the day it's there until you find a way to make peace. This is why so often people don't experience the grief process until years after a loved one passes, or they come from the stance, *I'll never get over this*.

The desire to feel better comes first. I couldn't imagine ever feeling happy again. My facilitator in my grief group shared that after her son passed, it took a while, but she did have times of happiness again. Even though I couldn't imagine feeling happy again, that gave me hope. It was possible for me, too.

Surrendering to what has happened comes next. We ease transitions first by accepting them, by accepting what is, what has happened, and not pushing against it in any way. Doing this allows enormous internal relief. I can feel it as I write it. If your loved one transitioned unexpectedly or violently, it can be a huge challenge. Just know there is nothing for you in the space of resistance in the pain. There is no need to hold on to anything longer than processing your emotions. It's not necessary to keep beliefs, judgments, or anything that is going to hamper your releasing resistance. Crying is good; cry as much as you can. Crying moves resistant energy from your body. Take care of yourself; don't judge yourself, and don't judge how you're grieving. That's resistance, too. It hurts. Accept that it hurts.

After surrender, the next step in this process is *change*. There may be life circumstances that will need to change. And equally important will be the changes in habits of thought that will allow you to respond to the change from a new perspective. These changes will allow your new way of Being to support and serve you.

There is no way to feel loss, especially of a loved one, and feel better. A shift in perspective is the only way. A passing, if the person is very old and ill, is more acceptable to embrace. It's easier to move through this grief. Young people in their prime—healthy and vibrant—well, there is something very wrong with that situation. How can it be embraced? This is resistant thinking that serves no one. Consistent resistant thoughts over months and years can take a physical toll.

I was challenged. How could I be in integrity if I didn't find a way to find peace with this change in my life? It was the biggest task I'd ever faced. It was before me, and I didn't want any part it. That changed, too. I *wanted* to have wisdom and grace through this process. It was a turning point not only as an event in my life but as an opportunity to be someone I had never been before. I decided I wanted to be a loving mother to my son Ryan, to be present for him. I knew at the core of my being that my work would change. I didn't know *how*—only that it would.

Change is always an opportunity for growth. It's a symptom of growth. You change inside, and external events align with your change. It can be scary, the unknown, or feel like too much change happening at once. Change can also be fun; it can be an adventure. Life is an adventure—ups and downs. It happens to everyone. How you respond is what is important. During my change, my personal transformation, I knew how I wanted to be. At times it was a challenge; I would forget and find myself in a place contrary to my desire.

Embracing change is a form of self-love, letting go of things that don't serve you. In the case of Garrett passing, I had to change my thoughts and challenge my beliefs. I had to change the negative energy of my thoughts that were draining my very core. It's a form of self-love to change negative thoughts to loving thoughts that affect you. Grief is a process of negative emotions. It's also an opportunity for a core change within.

Your connection with others who have passed is natural. We're all energy, and energy doesn't go away. Who said that when people transition, they are unreachable? Why is it so hard for so many of us to trust our own knowing? Most want to believe that our loved ones are very much near and well, but there is so much fear around leaving our bodies. There is joy when we enter them and much celebration around the birth of a family member. Of course it's natural to miss people when they leave their body. It's not the same interaction; it's a transition, a rebirth. It doesn't have to be the drama that we turn it into. At the risk of sounding callous, if we as a culture had a supportive, loving view of passing, it would alleviate much of the drama and pain. Don't feel that something has gone wrong when in fact nothing has gone wrong. Know that all is well, that our loved ones have gone through a transition after having completed their mission in this life in that body. Changing your thinking changes your perspective.

The change comes with trusting your own guidance, your own knowing, what feels right to you. Trust the signs, the sense you get that your loved one is with you. Trust yourself more than well-meaning others. This is more than coming to peace with your loved one passing. It's an awakening to an entirely new way of being. When you trust yourself, when you choose to trust your own senses, your own guidance, you'll step into your power and away from being a victim of circumstances. You'll feel it; you'll know it with all the fiber of your being. It's not wishful thinking; it is tapping into Grace.

Grief, people passing, or a loss of any kind meets with a substantial amount of resistance. What if we could look at our loved one's passing as if he or she just graduated from college or received a huge promotion? This change means my loved one is moving on to his or her next level of growth. It's a celebration. This might seem like a huge stretch, but it is the truth, and at some point we always resonate with the truth. Our culture, instead of embracing transitioning, has ingrained in us that transitioning is the worst possible thing that could happen. Grief is emotions of resistance to unexpected or unwanted change in our lives. It tends to make us feel like victims. In other words, this is happening *to me* rather than happening *for me*. When you can do this, you become open to a new perspective and solutions.

How long you spend in this state of resistance is your choice. There is no script—right or wrong. It is based on how willing you are to be in a place of resistance to what is. What's behind change that you are resisting? What causes change, do you know? Growth. Growth is what causes change. When you grow, you change. You literally shift your vibration, and everything around you shifts as well. The change you're resisting is your own growth. You have a huge battle going on inside, which results in symptoms of bitterness, anger, stress, health problems—the list of negative effects can go on and on. In the story I shared about my conflict with my ex-husband, I was holding on to resistance to prove that he was lying; this was my need to be right. Once I surrendered to the situation, I changed it.

What about a loved one passing? Of course you can't control when others leave, but try to look at things from the broader perspective, and know that before you were born you agreed to this event happening in your life, at this time, for your own growth. Since you agreed to experience this situation for your spiritual growth, how long do you want to spend resisting your spiritual growth?

The passing of a loved one can lend itself to the ultimate feeling of powerlessness. A chapter in your life has come to a close, and it may be one that you do not feel you are ready to close. You are not ready to say good-bye to what was.

When you become willing to be open to the change that has occurred, you can begin the new chapter. Most think the new chapter is without your loved one, which is why it feels so bad. This is not so. The new chapter begins with your loved one present but in a new form. Your loved one is still in your life but coming to you from a new platform.

I have often joked that Garrett is with me more now than if he were in his body. If he were in his body, we would see each other and talk, but he was starting his own life, and it was already beginning to be different with him. I remember grieving when he moved out of the house. It was something I knew one day would come, and I missed everything about him. It was bittersweet. I loved seeing him grow up, and I loved the young man he was and was excited for him and his life.

I know he is around me much of the time. I feel or see him with me. When I want to talk to him, I do, by speaking his name in my mind or out loud. I feel him with me immediately. I would not have this kind of access to him if he were in his body. He would connect with me when he could, but it was not instantaneous like it is now. This is a change I embrace and appreciate.

We work together in a way I could have never dreamed of before. He has his sense of humor intact; his loving nature shines; and a wisdom comes through. I cherish our relationship. The love we have for each other has only grown deeper with my own understanding. There are not words to convey the love and appreciation I have for Garrett. He has helped me see the beauty in life, the connections, the reality that he is very much available to me and always will be. The love that connects us to our loved ones is never broken and can be accessed any time. This you will always have.

Chapter Twenty-Two

The Power of Language

Language shapes the way we think,
and determines what we can think about.
—Benjamin Lee Whorf

If the language of our culture around death was different, grieving the transitioning of our loved ones would be less painful on many levels. First, no one dies. We leave our bodies; it's that simple. We move on to another form. Think of it like changing your clothes. I love the way Esther and Jerry Hicks explain it in their book *Ask and It Is Given*:

> When the physical personality is complete for this time, then there is a withdrawal of focus. It is sort of like: Here you sit, and sometimes you go into a movie, and sometimes you come back out of the movie, but you are always the you that went into the movie, whether you are in the movie or not.

When I first read this, just days after Garrett transitioned, I felt instant relief and tried to hang on to this metaphor while I was grieving. It was easy for me to understand that he had just left the movie. That was all it was; he was not lost or unreachable. I think of it as if he stepped out for popcorn and calls me from the lobby. This thinking, reminding myself of this, helped me tremendously. It calmed me down when I began to think otherwise.

Until Garrett's passing I did not realize how painful, disempowering, and untrue our language is around passing. I doubt I would have paid attention and certainly would not have been as passionate about language around death if I had not experienced the passing of my own beautiful son. I know these terms are detrimental to the well-being of all of us. They're part of the collective, and we all know them. Most of us believe them, even though we may not realize it.

It's time to change this thinking—these beliefs, our very language. As we change there will be less pain, suffering, grief, and fear. It's a complete shift in perspective, one that is congruent with our knowing deep within the core of our being. I know it is counter to the current mainstream culture, but it's important. This is how I began to heal my grief. I looked at everything—my beliefs, thoughts, words, all of it. What I came to realize is that our very words in describing what happens are painful and untrue.

Death—It would be empowering to eliminate the word death from our vocabulary. Rather than an end of a life it's more accurate to think of death as an end of an era or change. In my grief group, when I said my son died, it was a painful statement. Saying he transitioned or had his rebirth feels much better. How does it feel to you as you read this? Does saying *transition* or *rebirth* feel better to you? Trust your own knowing on this, the part of you that feels the relief, not your head that might want to tell you something different. It's not that I'm trying to sugarcoat what has happened; it's not that at all. I am stating what is accurate, what is true. No one dies. We leave our body. We change form. But to say someone is dead or has died is completely inaccurate. What is accurate is that a transition has happened. It's like saying when our children go off to college, they die because you may not see them for a while. It's a similar thing. I also use the word *passed*, which most people understand. My meaning is, he passed through his body to the nonphysical. As with birth, we are passing into a body.

Begin to look at the transition as a new beginning. Doesn't that shift the energy? Feel the difference as you read and digest the new thought, that it's a new beginning. This thought has the power to remove the pain and fear about transitioning.

Children Shouldn't Die Before Their Parents and Untimely Passings—People passing feels unnatural to us and hurts because we believe we have to let our loved ones go. The worst thought, which seems universal, is that there is nothing more painful than the death of a child. I have come to know that children passing before their parents is quite common. Years ago, children were lucky if they made it past childbirth and childhood diseases. Children passing, although painful, was quite common. All the young people who have fought in wars were children of parents. We're sending our children out right now to war against our very own values, knowing many will leave their bodies. Children transitioning before their parents is not so uncommon, even though we like to think it is unnatural. It happens and it happens often. Children shouldn't die before their parents implies something happened that wasn't supposed to happen, as if there was a fluke in nature, as if God made a colossal mistake.

That's just not possible. Everything is in Divine order and Divine timing. It's always the Soul's choice when to transition, and that decision is made before incarnating. So, there is no mistake; nothing has gone wrong.

Loss—*Loss* does not serve us when referring to a loved one who has passed. Although we certainly miss them and it *feels* like loss, our loved ones are not lost—actually, far from it. Feelings of loss are natural. A change has occurred, and things won't be the same. Your life will be different. I'm not suggesting ignoring your feelings because it can *feel* like loss, but know your loved one is not lost. Your loved ones are with you when you are thinking of them. You feel even worse when you're thinking of them being lost. It's more empowering to say I have feelings of loss, and then remind yourself that your loved ones are with you in the moment, wanting you to know they are with you and OK.

Whenever I have said, "I've lost someone," I feel so much worse than acknowledging *I'm feeling loss*. There is a big difference in the energy. One feels more like a victim and the other is an accurate, empowered and self-aware statement.

Accident and Tragedy—These words were used to describe my son's passing. I also heard, *What a waste,* which hurt me to no end because my son was not tragic, and his life, or seeming life that was not lived in his body, was not a waste. These terms made me angry when I heard them, although I didn't fully understand why at the time. Now, I know there is no truth to any of it.

The belief that there are tragic accidents or tragedies is from a physical perspective. From a spiritual perspective, however, there is always perfection. No matter how unjust or tragic something may seem, it is not that way at all from the Divine's perspective. We only have our limited view and not the broader view. Sometimes things can be difficult to understand, but there is peace in knowing that nothing has gone wrong. All is unfolding in Divine order.

Try to use other words that more accurately describe what has happened, or speak in a way that owns your emotions. I was in a car crash earlier this year. I made a special point never to use the word *accident* because I know in my heart it wasn't an accident; it was a car crash.

I'll Never Get Over This—I've heard this statement a lot. Again, because many people seem to equate suffering with the depth of love for those who have passed, many people have *bought into* the belief that they need to suffer to show their love. Therefore, this statement might seem to be another way of expressing how deeply the person who passed was loved, when in fact, the only thing this expression insures is the continued pain for the person still in physical form.

My interpretation of the energy is, I'll always be wounded by the event that has taken place. This feels like a decision of powerlessness, a decision of choosing to feel pain for the remainder of one's days rather than looking for the opportunity, the gift that has been given in a profound way. It could be an opportunity to find peace to forgive, an opportunity for so many gifts, actually. To declare that you will choose to feel pain, rather than peace or love, is a missed opportunity. It is a choice that your loved one does not want you to choose. Remember, beliefs are just thoughts, and you can change your thoughts. When you carry this kind of pain through months and years, it colors other areas of your life. It can take its toll on your health and your overall emotional well-being. I heard Oprah quote Dr. Phil: "It's not time that heals all wounds; it's what you do with the time." I completely agree with him. What you do, how you think, what you choose, determines your quality of life.

Chapter Twenty-Three

Intuitive Connection

These bodies are perishable but the dwellers in these bodies are eternal, indestructible and impenetrable.
—The Bhagavad Gita

In early 2009, I was inspired to listen to Doreen Virtue's radio show. I first found her show in early 2006 and enjoyed what she had to share about angels. After Garrett transitioned, I listened to her show every week for months. It was helpful to hear her do mediumship readings for some of her callers. I hadn't listened to Doreen's show for quite a while, but I was guided to listen one afternoon when I was home working in my office. During her show, she shares her upcoming classes. This time she was offering a mediumship class, which I had never heard her offer before. I could feel excitement about the thought of the class. As she was talking about it, I looked at her website and found that it was going to be a very small class. I wanted to go. I was communicating with Garrett at this time on my own, but I wanted to be better and more confident with it. It sounded like fun, and the excitement at the thought of attending the class was one I had not felt in a long time.

Shortly after, I went to see an intuitive, and I mentioned Doreen's mediumship class during my reading. My feelings were confirmed that this would be a good class for me to take, but not only for the reason I was intending. My angels were inviting me, encouraging me, to take the class so that I could do readings for other people. They told me I would be a powerful medium because of my experience with Garrett. They told me I would be able to help other parents with their grief.

This was not at all what I had anticipated. It was never on my radar to do readings for others. I was asked if I would be willing to do this, and I was honored. My emotions overwhelmed me. The thought of being asked and being able to help others the way I had been helped was overwhelmingly beautiful; the thought brought me to tears. How could I not do this and help others as well? My life took on a profoundly deeper purpose and so did my intention with mediumship.

The course was held in Hawaii. I took Ryan with me and was looking forward to being there and sharing Hawaii with him. It was a special opportunity to be in a small class with an internationally known intuitive, one I admired and whose books I had read. I was ready for an exceptional experience. I knew Garrett was going to be helping me, and it was going to be fun.

When I arrived the first morning of class, I met a few of the students and began to realize that all but one other person besides me were already professionals doing this type of work. I decided to put any fears I had aside and not let my ego get in the way. I knew I was supposed to be in the class. Everything had opened up for me to attend.

The first exercise for our class was listening for names. We each wrote a list of names that came to us. After we had completed our lists, we each shared with the entire group the names that we had heard. The rest of the class listened and acknowledged if the name of a person was their friend or loved one in the nonphysical. It was amazing and fun to see who all was there. I was surprised at some relatives who were there and even a parent of a friend. When it was my turn to list names, of course on my list was Garrett. I'd heard it clearly. When I got to his name I wasn't expecting a response because I knew he was there with me. What did surprise me was, a couple seats away from me, another participant who I had just briefly talked to before class said she'd heard Garrett too but discounted it because she has a son named Garrett. This was a wonderful learning experience for both of us. I felt like I had received confirmation. I wasn't imagining Garrett being there, and it was good for her to trust what she heard. She was right on. It had nothing to do with her Garrett at that time. Our son's connections later became clear.

The course was intense. The first afternoon we each gave a reading to someone in front of the class. This was intimidating to me but also empowering. I knew it was the best way for me to get started. I'm so thankful for Doreen creating the class in this manner. I gave my first reading to a woman who was second- or third-generation intuitive and very experienced in this arena. I had connected with a member of her family as had a classmate, which intimidated me because that person had already given her reading. When my turn came, I shared what I received from the same nonphysical person. My classmate was lovely and open as I shared information from her relative. I felt at ease as I shared what I received. She was able to confirm and put into context the information shared. I was excited, encouraged, and appreciative.

The class continued over the next several days of intense learning. I had the expectation, the feeling, that somehow Garrett would do something special while I was in the class. He had shown up at different times in readings to help. It was great and I appreciated it, but it was not on the scale that I thought he might show up. The last day of class our test for certification was to do a gallery-style reading similar to the first day and to get specific information from the nonphysical loved one to share. We were given a microphone and had to stand up in front of the class to share the name received. The person who was connected to that name stood and received the reading.

Keely, the woman whom I had met on the first day, whose son was also named Garrett, went up for her turn. She had the microphone, looked at me, and said "Garrett." I stood up and Keely began her reading. What she shared I could barely absorb. I was so amazed with both her and him. She told me that she had a paper cut out of a butterfly with her son Garrett's name on it. It had been on his locker at school. She said she had a sense, a feeling that she was supposed to bring it with her on the trip. She handed it to me. Prior to the trip, I had been seeing yellow and black butterflies that I never saw around my house before, and I knew they were from Garrett. I shared this with her. Then she gave me a package of M & M candies for Garrett's brother because he had told her it was Ryan's favorite candy, which it is. And, he wanted his little brother to know that he is always watching over him. Although she didn't know at the time that Garrett had been hit by a train as his *mode of transition*, she shared that Garrett had given her the symbol of a train. The message was to tell me that "You are on the right track. Don't doubt your knowing and your Truth." And to know that, "Each time you hear a train whistle, this is a reminder of his love and connection with you..." We were both in tears by the time she finished my reading. It was so amazing and fun to discover why she had been *encouraged* to bring the butterfly from Michigan to Hawaii—even before we had made any physical connection *here*. I had no idea he was working on our connection to meet so far in advance. Garrett loves surprises and connections. He sure surprised us! We were so overjoyed with his work in connecting us. This is the kind of experience I expected he would do, something really special. He went all out. I couldn't have been happier, and I don't think Keely could have been either. She did a fantastic job listening to Garrett. What a blessing, as we have become close friends and colleagues.

My turn to give a reading came later in the day, which was good. It gave me time to get grounded after the special connection with Garrett and Keely. When we came back from lunch, I mentally asked to hear a name. Rather quickly I saw the name spelled out. When it was my turn, I said that I had the name, and I spelled it out because it was a name that could be for a man or a woman—but is spelled differently according to gender. Much to my surprise, and some nervousness, it was Doreen who knew this person in nonphysical. She was gracious and shared that the same thing had happened to her when she first learned mediumship. She offered to let me do a reading for someone else if I was nervous. I told her I would be fine. I knew that I was supposed to do this reading. It went well and I received my certification. It was a huge validation for me and my capabilities. I had given accurate information to my instructor, someone I looked up to and admired for her work and integrity.

My class experience was everything I had hoped for and more. I not only received my certification, but I also met new friends and colleagues.

In my intuitive work, there are many benefits. One that is particularly special is that I easily feel the love that comes through messages from loved ones who have passed.

Many believe that once someone has transitioned, it is not possible to connect with that person again. There are also many others who don't give this much thought, automatically believing the cultural norms. But when they experience the passing of a loved one, it opens the door to other possibilities.

A term I'm not a fan of is *medium*. To me it has a connotation of a charlatan or someone abnormal. The entire point of the book is that tapping into your intuitive knowing is normal. What is abnormal and gets you into trouble is ignoring it, pretending it doesn't exist. I also struggle with the term *reading*. Even though reading is an interpretation, the word *connection* feels more accurate. It's an acknowledgement and connection with your intuition and loved ones in nonphysical.

When my grandfather passed in 2000, I felt him and talked to him. I felt him quite a bit when he first passed, while I was driving, for example, or at home when I was cleaning, when my mind was uncluttered and open. I would sense him, sense his energy, and I talked to him. It felt good. I knew my grandfather was with me, letting me know he was present.

I know now, because of the work that I do, that many people have this experience with a loved one who has passed. Even though I couldn't see my grandfather, I could feel him and communicate with him. This is normal. If we all acknowledged, embraced, and encouraged continued relationships after transitioning, imagine how different our culture would be, how much the fear of leaving our bodies would diminish. It's time to realize that what most think of as extraordinary is *ordinary*. Your world changes when you pay attention to the gifts and love that are within you and around you now. Relationships don't end; they continue and can grow stronger, if we pay attention and allow the connection, just as if the person was still in the body. This is what I know to be true because it has happened to me in my relationship with my son.

In the book *Hello From Heaven!*, authors Bill and Judy Guggenheim stated that 67 percent of people who have had a loved one pass have felt or had some type of connection with their loved one. If you haven't already, you can too, if you have a strong desire and believe it's possible.

Many scoff at the possibility of connecting with loved ones. It takes courage to speak up to the contrary, but many are doing it. I'm reminded of my time with my grief group. After I spoke up and shared my feeling of Garrett's presence with me, others began to share their stories of connections. Many people directly connect with their loved ones regularly; they just aren't always sure or aware of what's happening. There are different degrees of the level of communication, but the majority of the people I've worked with have felt their loved ones around them after their passing. But many are uncomfortable bringing this up.

Chapter Twenty-Four

Signs You Can Trust

In order to find the treasure, you will have to follow the omens.
—Paulo Coelho, The Alchemist

You are a multisensory being. Along with your five senses, you have more sophisticated senses as well. Once you have an awareness of them and a desire to tap into them, you open yourself to the world of the unseen, the world of nonphysical. This is nothing to fear. In this book, I want to focus on using your senses to connect with your highest self, to govern your intuition or instincts, and to connect with your loved ones in nonphysical.

What I've learned from connecting with loved ones who have transitioned is that they want you to know they are near you, happy, and that they can communicate with you. When you sense they are near, it's vital that you trust your deepest instincts, your own knowing. The biggest mistake you can make is discounting the feeling and the signs you receive as your imagination or wishful thinking. It's time to change your thinking, to stop thinking and begin to feel. Trust your feelings and your knowing, trust what you sense, and practice trusting your intuitive knowing.

We all like confirmation and validation, so I'll share some of my experiences because I'm sure you've had them, too. I hope sharing my experiences will help you identify your loved one connecting with you. I can't stress enough how important it is to trust your instincts. That's a big part of what you are here to do, and your loved ones are eager to help you. Try it; it's fun.

Garrett let me know he was around by running the water in the bathroom, flashing lights, and turning on battery-operated toys. I have also smelled scents of loved ones, you might smell perfume or even a cigarette, if someone who has passed smoked. It's a scent that you connect with them, and it's a sign they are near. Some move things around; our loved ones can be playful. You might hear songs on the radio that remind you of them. This happened to me all the time when Garrett first transitioned, and it still does. I'll hear a certain song and know it's from him. You might see numbers signifying their birthday, or some other special sequence, that your loved ones know will have meaning for you.

Upon reflecting on all the signs from Garrett, he's really interacted with us consistently, as if he never left—because, of course, he has not left. When I would lie in bed at night, I would feel the bed lightly shake. At first I wondered if it was my imagination or one of the dogs. I soon realized it was Garrett. It was like he was standing next to the bed, leaning over with both arms extended and his hands on the bed purposefully wiggling it. He did this often for quite some time. His doing this made me smile, and it comforted me.

Our loved ones in nonphysical can communicate through small children. Ryan would say things to me that didn't sound like a three-year-old; it sounded more like Garrett. He would go around the house pointing and saying G. One morning he was at the breakfast table, and I heard Ryan say, "This is my house." I asked him who he was talking to, and he said, "G." One day we were driving in the car, and he told me G was in the front passenger seat. Then, when Ryan was about five or six and running around the house, he said he was racing Garrett.

I also began to find little treasures around the house from Garrett. I had a book on angels that was in my office, and I hadn't read it in years. A few months after he passed, I opened it and inside was an old napkin with a drawing he drew of his dog, BJ, him, and me. I had forgotten all about it. Things like this popped up and still do. One of my favorites is seeing a picture of him I've never seen before. I love it. I thought I'd never see a new picture of him, and now every so often a new one shows up from someone. It's a treat and always feels like a gift from Garrett because he knows how fun it is for me. I experience the same joy when Ryan picks a bouquet of daisies for me.

I have found cards Garrett had made for me, little scribbles he had drawn. These little treasures that come across my path are a surprise and always feel like a special gift.

Dreams are often talked about as a sign you've had a visit from a loved one. It took me awhile to have a vivid dream of Garrett that I could remember. In the first dream, we were in his bedroom having a conversation about me making him a sandwich. Even though I was still sleeping, I realized that he had transitioned while I was talking to him. I was happy he was with me. The dream was about an everyday conversation. It wasn't like, "Where have you been?" When I woke, I was still happy and realized the everydayness of it was his way of showing me he's with me all the time—that it's no big deal he's in nonphysical now.

When you have a vivid dream and your loved ones appear, trust that it is them. It's often one of the easiest ways for your loved ones to connect with you because you become open in the dream state. If you receive a dream and your loved ones are not happy with you, check in with yourself. Do you have guilt or judgment about the situation in the dream? I had a friend whose husband had passed, and she said she dreamed that he was mad at her because she remarried and was happy. This was not her husband being mad at her; this was her guilt for being happy again. Your loved one would never come to you from any place but love. Feel it. You know the truth will resonate with you. Remember, guilt comes from a place of fear.

One year for Mother's Day, I started to order flowers for my mother. I was online beginning to place the order, and I chose a different gift altogether for my mother. I was going to log out when I heard Garrett start to sign the card, and it was to me. I realized he was the one wanting to send flowers to me on Mother's Day. I thought it was so sweet of him, and I said it was OK. I knew his intention. I didn't need the flowers and cancelled the order. To my surprise I received a dozen beautiful roses on Mother's Day with the card from Garrett. I called the florist who said there had been a mistake. They could see the order had been cancelled and told me to keep the flowers at no charge. Garrett sent me flowers on Mother's Day four years after he transitioned. It brings tears to my eyes as I write this; he's always been thoughtful.

Animals can also be influenced. Birds are often easily influenced by our nonphysical loved ones. During the first connection I had with a medium, Garrett had shown himself as a hawk watching me. Within the first year of his passing, a friend of mine e-mailed me. She said she saw the Pink Floyd video *Learning to Fly*, and she had thought of Garrett. This was his way of communicating to her.

On a couple of occasions, I've seen a red-tailed hawk in my backyard. The first time I saw it, it was perched on the fence. I was in the backyard, and this huge bird landed on the fence while I was standing just a few feet away. I see hawks flying around the area frequently, but I'd never seen one land in the middle of a suburban neighborhood. I knew it was from Garrett. About a year later, I saw another red-tailed hawk in my backyard, but this time it was perched on the deck rail within a few feet of the house. I knew it was also from Garrett.

Garrett continues to connect with me in fun ways that make me smile. Garrett has introduced me to many wonderful people, and he still teases me like he did when he was in his body. When I am working in my office, sometimes I'll see the plant move as if someone has flicked the leaves with his or her finger. He does many little things, just as if he were in his body. Without a doubt, he's done many things for me and others that I am not aware of, but I love when he does something dramatic to say, "Hello."

About two years after Garrett passed, my parents were on vacation and ran into a man who was very upset. They began talking to him and he shared that his son Garrett had recently passed. After their conversation with this stranger my mother immediately called me to share the story. She knew when the man said his son's name it was a message from her grandson Garrett she could feel him.

A similar situation happened to Garrett's friend Joe and me. We were having dinner and a woman he worked with came to our table to say hello. When Joe and I were leaving, we stopped at her table to say goodbye. She was with her husband and son, who she introduced as Garrett. We immediately glanced at each other knowing it was a hello from Garrett.

If, out of nowhere, you begin to think of your loved one, it's your loved one connecting with you, letting you know that he or she is with you.

Garrett's friends tell me they feel him around. At times I challenge them a little and ask them how they know it was Garrett. The answer is always, "I just know it's him." I know it's him, too. I have friends who never met Garrett when he was in his body, but they say they have felt him around. When this first happened, it made my heart sing to know that Garrett was with my new friends and that they recognized him, without ever meeting him in his physical body. It's exciting that he is not only present with me and Ryan, but that he is also interacting with our friends as well, and they know it, too. My knowing is affirmed that even though the form changes, Consciousness does not go away. We can still have relationships with our loved ones in nonphysical.

When I was grieving and going through my legal drama, my dear friend Paula called me and told me she received a message for me from Garrett and an angel. She had last seen Garrett when he was eleven-years-old. Paula heard a message and wrote it down for me. It was literally a gift from heaven at the time, a lifeline for me. When I asked how she knew it was Garrett, she said she just knew. Here is the message that she received:

> Tell my mom that I'm OK, that I'm where I'm supposed to be. I'm where I chose to be. This is all part of the plan. There's a bigger picture here that's unfolding. Tell her it's OK to miss me but not to be sad for me. I'm not missing out on anything. I'm free. I love it. This is so much better and intense than what I experienced before. Tell her not to worry about me and not to regret or feel bad about when I was there with Josh. I knew how to handle it. She can't see me when she dreams because I'm right there beside her. She can't see me or hear me because it's not part of the plan. She won't be able to, so don't be disappointed. That's something that she chose as well. Just know that I'm there. I can see her. I love her and know she loves me. She has the strength to get through this. With me gone and the stuff with Josh I'll be watching my little brother. I'm not cocky, just good looking.

It's interesting to know that Garrett referred to the mystical experience he'd had when he said, "This is so much better and intense than what I experienced before." My friend had no knowledge of this when she received this message. I would oftentimes feel sad for Garrett, feeling like he was missing out on things—hence, his reference to not feeling sad and seeing everything. Again, not something that I shared with others. I also felt badly about things that had happened with my ex-husband, as more things had been revealed to me after we divorced. I couldn't understand why I wasn't having the vivid dreams with Garrett. Others had shared with me that they were having dreams with Garrett, and I was questioning why I wasn't. This message helped me understand the bigger picture. I wanted to see him in form, standing in the room with me, not just in my mind's eye. The reference to being cocky was aimed at my friend receiving the message. She was always telling me she could feel Garrett around, that he had kind of a cocky energy. Of course, his sense of humor would come through as well.

Even though this book is not about angels, I work with angels and try to remember to call upon them often for help. It warms my heart that an angel also came through for me, really for all of us, as this came during my challenges with Ryan's father. I had been asking for help, and there was a loving answer.

The angel's message helped me; the message made it easy for me to pray for Josh, which would have been a stretch before the message. To be honest, before the message, I was hoping he'd get run over by a truck or something. Quite likely, he felt the same about me.

The key is to pay attention to the signs. It's easy to be distracted and miss the signs. Next, it is important to trust your intuition, your own knowing. My friend Paula trusted her intuition and wrote down the message from Garrett. You probably have more than one loved one who has transitioned, and if you have the sense one is around, ask yourself this question: "How do I know this is…" See what comes to you.

Fear or guilt sometimes surfaces when I am working with people. They have some anxiety about connecting with a loved one. The anxiety is usually about some fear or guilt the person is carrying. This can be about a lifestyle, how the relationship was when the person passed, or any unresolved issue.

If you have felt this, it's important that you know that there is nothing that you could do or could have done that would keep your loved ones from connecting with you. What they want you to know is that the opposite is true. They want you to let yourself off the hook. Guilt is not necessary. Its source is of the ego and has no place when connecting with loved ones. This is heart-to-heart, Soul-to-Soul communication. It is a place of unconditional love. You may not be feeling unconditional love in the moment with loved ones, but they are holding it for you. When they left their body, they left all the resistance they were carrying as well. This is why they feel so good, why they hold no grudges, why they want to support and help you to know there is no death or loss and no need to grieve a minute longer than necessary.

Sometimes a person who has passed may have done harm to someone still in his or her physical body. There is a fear by the client wanting to connect with someone else, that this person will come through. The person who passed probably does want to come through to try to give peace to the situation, but I have found there is always respect of the wishes of the client, and so this person does not intrude if my client is not ready for this conversation. In time, most clients do find a time when they are ready to connect with this person. They have worked through their issue and are ready to hear what the passed person has to say. It's an opportunity for peace. The person who has passed sees from a new perspective and will come from a place of love and responsibility. He or she has compassion.

When I returned home from Hawaii, more connections began to happen. While I was sharing my experience in Hawaii with a coaching colleague, I felt her mother with us, her mother who passed many years ago.

Her mother had loving messages for her. It was completely unexpected. I wasn't trying to connect with her mother. This was a moment to cherish for my colleague and her mother. I was fortunate enough to be in the energy of this love.

This happens fairly often, as loved ones in the nonphysical will try to get through any opportunity they can find, like Garrett did with my friend during her date. This began to happen to me quite often and still does. If I'm not with the person I'm receiving the message for, I write it down and share it with them. It's like a phone call from the loved one, and I'm taking a message.

This is perhaps the sweetest part of my work: every time I prepare to work with someone, I ask Garrett to work with me. I know he's already with me, waiting for me, but I ask for his assistance. It's particularly special working together when I connect with a loved one for a client.

My intuitive business has evolved. When I first started, I wasn't sure how it was going to look. I already had a career and leadership development coaching practice and felt that if people in that arena knew I was using my intuitive guidance, I would lose credibility. Even though I was using my intuitive abilities, I didn't directly share this with my clients. I feared people would think I was weird, too *out there*. My corporate friends agreed with my assessment that I would lose credibility. For several years I kept the two businesses separate, except I let my intuitive clients know I had a coaching practice.

As I began my intuitive practice, it quickly became clear my coaching skills complemented the intuitive work, and I often combined a bit of coaching in these sessions. There was opportunity in each session for people to have a deeper, even more meaningful experience.

After a couple of years, maintaining two practices was beginning to become a burden. I was passionate about my work and knew that it was time to blend my practices into one business. I was afraid at first, but knew I had to overcome my fear of what others might think of me. It made sense that, as I grow, my work was going to grow with me. My work in both practices was all about change and embracing all of it.

I spoke to a public relations expert about my concerns, and in that discussion she said, "You know there are many people in the corporate world who are in the closet with this." I knew she was right. I was one of them. I was afraid I would lose the opportunity to work with corporations in helping them with leadership and transition. In honor of my own authenticity, so be it. It was incredibly freeing to let go of my fears of judgment about what those in the corporate world might think. I soon realized that even my corporate clients were on a spiritual path and my being authentic only enhanced my credibility.

There are leadership programs that are beginning to address instincts, of following them, and of breaking through limiting beliefs. They are saying the same thing but seem to be afraid to mention spirituality. Yet, that's what it is; instinct is another word for intuition. For some reason, people tend to be uncomfortable with intuition and more comfortable with instinct. It doesn't matter; it is the same thing. For me, it has become important to be comfortable to say that it's all spiritual. Everything physical is spiritual. Just because something can't be seen doesn't mean it doesn't exist, and once you begin to open up to this, many other limiting beliefs can be challenged and a new way of looking at life becomes clearer and clearer. It then allows you to accept your sensing of your loved ones around you—because they are; it allows you to trust your own knowing, your instincts on everything in your life. You begin operating on a multisensory level, which we all are capable of doing.

I had many intuitive clients from the corporate world. My practice is now what I envisioned it to be, helping others through change and transition and combining all of my skills and abilities to support others to do the same. We're all in this together, to help each other be the best of who we are.

CHAPTER TWENTY-FIVE

Multi-Senses

He realized: If I can learn to understand this language without words, I can learn to understand the world.
—Paulo Coelho, The Alchemist

We are all aware of our five senses: sight, sound, touch, taste, and smell. Lesser-known senses are:

- Clairvoyance—Sight;
- Clairsentience—Feeling;
- Clairaudience—Hearing; and
- Claircognizance—Knowing.

You may or may not be aware that you have them. That was me. I was using these senses all my life and, most of the time, was not present to them. I didn't have a clear understanding of these senses or a desire to cultivate them. I have had many clients who were just like me: not present and a bit ignorant of multi-senses.

I mentioned earlier we are vibration. It's understood that we interpret our five senses through vibrations; our clairs interpret higher vibrations.

There is a story about Aborigines that had never seen a ship. In the story, there is a ship in the harbor, and no one could see it because none of them had ever seen a ship before. They couldn't comprehend it was even there. Then, one day, one of them saw the ship, and then more in the tribe began to see the ship, too. Once it was perceived and communicated, it was possible for all to see the ship.

We are not conditioned to believe we can see angels, but that does not mean they are not all around us. Digital camera technology now captures them in photos; they show angels are very much around. Next time you look through your family photos, look for the orbs. I am sure you will see them.

It's hard to explain how I receive this higher vibrating information from the nonphysical. Sometimes, I receive information in several different ways all at once, and I do my best to interpret what I'm receiving. It's a similar challenge to try to describe an event like a basketball game that you are watching. How do you describe how your eyes interpret the vibration of sight? You just see the court, the players, the ball, the baskets, the referees—they are just there. How do you describe how you hear the crowd cheering? You just hear it; you don't know *how* your ears do it—you only know the result. It's the same thing with interpreting nonphysical energy. It's hard to describe; it's just there. At a basketball game, for example, there are many things going on all at once. You are automatically interpreting without conscious thought. It's all happening in real time. You're aware of the game, the arena, the food vendors, the other fans, but you're not trying to describe it all at once. All the feelings being conveyed are instantly interpreted by you. This is the best example I can think of in describing the nonphysical energy. I can just interpret it. I don't really understand how it works, just as I couldn't begin to tell you how my ears interpret the sound waves into voices that I understand; it's an automatic interpretation.

Connecting with the high-vibrating energy requires strong desire, intention, belief it is possible, and awareness. Our clairs are a more refined version of our senses. When I felt my grandfather with me after he passed, I felt him but didn't realize how clairsentient I was. I didn't even know the word clairsentience. I was aware of him and the sweet connection, but I wasn't completely present to myself in this ability of connection, even though it was as automatic as my eyesight.

Garrett helped me remember events when writing this book. He showed me where the message he gave my friend Paula was located.

I'm going to give a brief description of each of the clairs. As you read them, take a minute to reflect and notice which of these you already use on a regular basis. How present have you been to them?

Clairvoyance—Clairvoyance is seeing nonphysical energy. This energy can come in different forms. It can be seen as apparitions, orbs, sparkles, light, movement of energy or blurriness, and it can be pictures or visions in your mind's eye.

When I was little, I could see colored sparkles around, and I have since learned that this is angelic energy. For many years I forgot that I used to see sparkling energy all the time when I was a child.

Until Garrett passed, I thought being clairvoyant meant only seeing apparitions. I clearly saw the apparition of our dog BJ in my bedroom after he passed. Another time when I was tucking Ryan into bed, I saw a good-sized orb about eight inches in diameter. It was a beautiful shade of purple. I watched it for almost a minute. I would look away and look back, and it was still there. I was familiar with orbs because I had recently seen them in photographs. It was exciting to me that I was seeing the nonphysical so clearly. I had the desire and I had been asking to see in this way.

What I hadn't been aware of until about four months after Garrett passed is that each time I had seen him in my mind's eye, I was experiencing another type of sense, clairvoyance. I was seeing him in the same way I had seen the dog and the orb. Learning this changed my landscape. It brought me great joy to know that we were connecting all along. I was seeing him. I wished I had known earlier the different sights of clairvoyance. Before I moved to Tahoe, I had a vision that came to fruition. It was just as interesting to share this with my mother to find out she, too, sees clairvoyantly—and didn't know that's what was happening.

Clairsentience—Clairsentience is feeling, the ability to feel energy. Have you ever walked into a room and you could tell that the people already in the room—even though they were not speaking—were upset with each other? How did you know this? You were feeling the energy around you, and you could feel their anger or frustration. No one had to speak. How about when someone says one thing but you can feel the exact opposite exuding from his or her energy? Have you ever been in a situation where something or someone just didn't feel right? You just had a "bad feeling" about where you were or who was around you. You might have called it a "bad vibe." This is clairsentience; there is a feeling.

When someone says something, and you get the chills or goose bumps, this is also clairsentience. When I feel this, it is always a confirmation of a truth. I often feel these when I'm working with a client, and they confirm we are on the right track.

Many times I have felt touched. It can be a hug or a hand on the shoulder. I often can see or feel when a client's loved one is giving him or her a hug, and I'll ask my clients if they can feel it. Usually they do.

Clairsentience is also that gut feeling, the feeling you get when you just know the right decision to make.

An example that many people experience is thinking of someone and then receiving a phone call or some other communication from him or her. You're sensing that person's energy.

When I experienced extreme tightness in my chest prior to Garrett's passing, it was clairsentience.

You might feel a pressure change, similar to the feeling you sometimes get while traveling on an airplane. This is angelic presence.

You might have had the experience where someone walked in your front door or in your office at work. You don't see that person at first but you feel the energy and know who is there. In this case, you're recognizing the person's energy. This is the energy we know each other by. It's a great example of recognizing our individual life force. You recognize someone before you see that person. When a loved one passes, it's the same energy—just in the nonphysical without the form of a body.

As an empath, I could feel others' sadness when they would hear about Garrett. I feel other people's responses to my story, which are the emotions they carry about themselves, just like when I used to feel so bad for the parents of Garrett's friends who had passed. I've had to learn to let this flow through me, rather than hang on to it.

Clairaudience—This is hearing. You might hear your voice, or someone else's. It can be inside you or outside you. You might even hear sounds. I hear tones that are often combined with the pressure change. If you hear tones, pay attention to what is happening in that exact moment; the tone could be highlighting a message for you. Pay attention to what was recently happening because it might be an answer to a question you have. These are always loving, helpful messages or maybe even a sound. For quite some time after Garrett passed, I would hear a train. This was Garrett's way of letting me know he was with me.

You may hear a song that resonates, something on TV, or a conversation with a friend. These are all ways of messages getting to you.

Claircognizance—Claircognizance is a knowing. It's information that you just know. I like to think of it as being downloaded like a computer. This is one of my primary forms of receiving information with my clairs. It's why I didn't realize that I knew things others did not. I can receive information about people when I meet them. I receive information by their energy. It's more than how they feel, which is clairsentience. It is a combination I receive simultaneously.

Often I would share information with friends, and they would challenge me on how I could know. I didn't know how I knew, I just did. This is claircognizance.

Notice how you receive information. Pay attention. If you're not aware of using your multi-senses, you can set an intention to notice when you're using your clairs. Notice what ones are predominant. You can set an intention to strengthen these senses as well.

Here's where most people get tripped up: the energy can be faint. It tends to go unnoticed or is disregarded because of its subtlety. You might think, "Oh, it's my imagination or wishful thinking." That's why your loved ones tend to do things like flash lights, run water, or find others who can relay a message on their behalf. They are trying as loud as they can to get your attention.

Before Garrett's transition, he and I would have conversations, and I would tell him, "I was sending you love today. Did you feel it?" Garrett would tell me he could. I would tell him, "I felt like you were having a difficult time." He would confirm this, too. Garrett did the same with me. He would say, "Mom, I was thinking of you and sending you love. Could you feel it?" This was a few years before we had the conversation about trying to communicate without talking and being in different places. We were already aware of our connection. Our discussion about telepathy and to practice communicating this way was taking our multi-sensory communication to the next level.

After he transitioned, I didn't know if I could continue to directly communicate with him. Even though I could feel him so close at times, my fearful mind would tell me he was far away. After he transitioned, my desire to talk to him and receive clear messages from him was so strong, there was no bucking the current. It was going to happen. When I spent time with his body, and I felt him so strongly and could hear him talk to me, it was grounding and joyful, an experience that gave me a strength and a knowing, even though I still had to get my arms around the whole event. *He's here but not* took some time to reconcile.

Your loved ones are cheering for you to be aware so you can clearly connect with them. Ask them to help you with his process; they are eager to do so. Trust what you receive. If you're not sure, ask them to give you a sign that you will know without a doubt that it is them. It's important to ask them in this way. Some people want a specific answer or sign, and this doesn't work for a couple of reasons. First, it's important to be open. When you're looking for a sign that you designate, you're not open and miss what is being shown to you. Your loved one may have a more important message, a better sign, or something humorous to share. If you're not open to what is being shared, you miss the treasure. The point is to be developing your senses and awareness, but this doesn't happen if you try to dictate and control the content and/or circumstances of communication. Dictating the *what* and *how* is controlling; it's grounded in fear, and you won't achieve the desired results from this stance.

If you have questions you'd like to ask, this is great, but be open to the answer. You may get answers you're not expecting and think that it did not come from your loved one. This is not the case. Your loved one has a broader view, a bigger perspective on things, and the answer you receive will come from this perspective—not the one that you might expect. Do expect humor. I find that our loved ones after they transition retain their sense of humor and are more lighthearted than they were when they were in their bodies.

The first time I talked to Garrett with a medium, I asked what happened when he transitioned. He didn't want to talk about it or focus on it. He said to think of his body like a rag doll, not him. He was right. Focusing on what happened only made me feel worse. I find the same thing with others who have passed. There are times when I work with the loved ones who want to know more details about the physical aspect of the passing. Their nonphysical loved ones don't like to focus on it because the way they exit their bodies isn't important. For those of you who have experienced a loved one who committed suicide, or was murdered, this may be hard. Your loved ones are not bitter or depressed. They no longer have any negative feelings about leaving, and if a perpetrator was involved, they are not holding on to a grudge. It doesn't matter to them. We're the ones who make the exit a big deal. Your loved ones are in a state of grace. They don't feel the anger, judgment, and fears that we do. They want you to know this because they see how much grief, guilt, and anger this causes so many. They love us and want us to feel peace rather than anguish. They understand our human feelings, of course, but they want you to know you make it much harder than it needs to be. Shifting your perspective will give you the peace you want.

With some clients, I can feel their family members with them, even though my clients are not ready to engage with them yet. It's OK. There is no judgment, only love and understanding from the nonphysical. If you feel like you do want to move into a different place on a subject but are not ready to connect with the person, setting an intention to be open to moving to a place that serves your highest good would be a good start in shifting your energy. If you've been deeply betrayed or wronged in some way and want to release the energy you are feeling so you no longer feel angry, resentful, hurt, or victimized, then this intention is a good first step. The important thing is for you to begin to feel better and release any negative energy within you. Releasing this energy does not mean that what this person did was OK. It releases the power you have given him or her over you. In essence you take your power back. This may have been the entire reason for the event or actions that took place—to help you learn to step in to your power no matter what. It is something powerful to know, that no matter what happens, you can stay in your power.

This is self-love. Any thought you have that isn't of love is damaging to your well-being. All fearful thoughts muck with your vibration, your health. You feel it as anxiety or stress, and from there it can manifest in your life in many different ways. It's so important to begin the process of changing fearful thoughts to loving thoughts.

It's no different with grief. Grief, at its root, is one fearful thought after another. It can be a visceral feeling. When you can begin to change these fearful thoughts into loving, empowered thoughts, your healing can begin. Your life takes on a new meaning and perspective, and you will never be able to go back to the old way of thinking.

Often, when someone first passes, you're in an extreme state of grief and very low vibration, while your loved one has just left his or her body and is vibrating at a high level. At first, while you're in a grief stricken place, you may not be able to hear or sense your loved ones. Don't panic! It doesn't mean they aren't near you. It just means you can't hear them, but it will pass. If you set an intention that you want to connect with them it will happen. It did for me and has brought many gifts to me and others.

During one of my readings with Garrett, I was sobbing, missing him. He was present, relaxed, not judging me, but motioning with his arm and his hand—sort of beckoning. He was motioning this way, saying, "Come on; get it all out." His demeanor was relaxed and casual, as if I were crying over a sad movie or a minor disappointment. It calmed me and helped me to put what had happened into perspective. He wasn't judging my crying, but he wasn't babying me either. He was present and understanding, and I felt like he would be there with me while I went through my grief process. And he was, in a way that was respectful—loving and in good humor. This is how he has been with me ever since. Some of Garrett's friends were having a difficult time with his passing, and I asked him what would he like his friends to know? He said think of it as if he were living in a different state. This made good sense to me. We can still communicate with someone living in a different state, even though we are not physically present with each other.

When you've decided to be open to connection with your loved ones, just relax. Trying too hard can create resistance and block connection. Set your intention and trust when you sense a connection.

Chapter Twenty-Six

Gifts in Transitioning

Remember that wherever your heart is, there you will find your treasure. You've got to find the treasure, so that everything you have learned along the way can make sense.
—Paulo Coelho, The Alchemist

Garrett's transition was a catalyst for a profound spiritual awakening. Having my heart broken wide open allowed for my awakening to a new way of being. For the first time I could embrace the multi-sensory being that I am. I made the choice to acknowledge and claim this part of me.

Garrett's passing gave me an opportunity to challenge my beliefs on a level I didn't know existed. It brought me to own who I am and what I know. It has given me the courage to speak my truth and become more of my authentic self. There is a peace within me that is the transforming spiritual shift. My entire landscape changed, which could not have happened without Garrett's passing. There is no way that a lesser event could have inspired me to do the work I love at such depths.

This was the agreement Garrett and I had. I would experience his transition so that I could share it with you. Before Garrett passed, he was on his way to sharing this message. He had figured it out. He is sharing this message with me; we're doing this together. I had a dream that we would work together, and it's happening. We are working together in a way that I could have never anticipated, but at the deepest level of my being. I am continuing to learn and grow with each experience, as I'm sure this is the beginning. There will be more to learn and share.

When the focus is on death and loss, you cannot move through the grief process and achieve peace. When you begin to look at what has happened as an opportunity for your expansion, your spiritual awakening, you open the door to a new perspective. It is an expansion that literally cracks your heart wide open so that pain and fear can be released. They are replaced with peace and a light that shines. It's a chance to connect with the Divine in a deeper way, to feel the love that is always here for us. When you connect in this way, it's easy to let go of all the minor irritations in life. This deeper connection to your Soul allows a peace and a knowing inside. It's comforting for me to know that I never will go back to the way I was before. I cried deeply because things would never be the same again. I was mourning the past and the future I had anticipated. I didn't want to move forward without Garrett in his body. This resistance depleted me. I felt completely disconnected from God. It was the darkest feeling I have ever experienced.

A new way to connect and grow was the option I chose. This completely changed my outlook. It was painful and took many hours of practice to change. When I first heard the idea of changing my thoughts, I thought it was impossible. I learned otherwise. I could change my thoughts. My motivation was my need for peace, as everywhere I looked I had none. It's OK and healthy to feel the pain and move through it. The key is to keep moving and not stay stuck in one area. That's the danger of taking medication for too long, or self-medicating with alcohol or other recreational drugs. It masks the pain, and then you haven't really moved through the process.

My heart being broken was my chance to elevate my well-being and to see the gift of continuing my relationship with Garrett in nonphysical.

The opportunity—the gift—your loved one has given you is the opportunity for you to learn and tap into your own spirituality on a deeper level, to know that your loved one is not gone but has only left his or her body. The body is not the person you know and love. Think of your body as an outfit you wear. It's not you; it's what you're wearing. I often hear older people say they feel younger than they are. I believe this is because we are not our bodies; our life force is youthful. We are eternal beings. When you know this, it changes your entire outlook.

As I look back on the events of our lives before Garrett transitioned, I can see the perfection of the timing, how everything was beautifully orchestrated for his transition. He was very happy. He had connected with many loved ones he had not seen in a while.

I feel that I am helping him, that we are a team, and that we signed up to be a team at this time to share a message. The work he wanted to do before he transitioned is being done, and it's with me—he in nonphysical and me in physical. It's the best of both worlds. We have a story to tell, important things to share that can help you ease your grief, find peace, and tap into the love and Grace that surrounds you. It's all here right now; there is no need to wait.

It's important to trust your own knowing, to trust what you sense. If you share your experience with others and they disregard your connection, it's time to decide who you are going to believe—you, your own guidance, or someone who has no understanding and is disconnected. This is one of the gifts in your loved one's transition, the opportunity to be aware of your internal guidance, your higher self, to know that no one dies.

The gifts I have received from Garrett are many. I am sure I am not fully aware of all of them yet. Thus far, this is what I have learned:

- We do not die
- No one is lost
- Our loved ones are with us
- Our loved ones are happy
- Our connection of love is never broken
- We choose our parents
- Our loved ones will help us
- I can choose peace and joy over pain and sorrow
- I am much more than I thought
- I can directly connect with those in nonphysical form
- Our culture promotes victimization and loss
- We are safe
- Spiritual perspective transforms grief
- There are no untimely passings
- Life-changing events are for our spiritual awakening
- My beliefs and thinking control the way I feel

We Do Not Die—This is the paradigm shift that changes everything. Once you really believe this, life is never the same. Life becomes easier; you feel free; and pain is replaced by relief. Some may say this is just wishful thinking. That's OK; some are not yet ready for a new reality. You, on the other hand, are ready. You have had an experience that has led you to this book, and you know deep in your heart the paradigm of death is incorrect. The truth is, there is only life.

No One is Lost—While you may have feelings of loss, no one is lost. Loved ones are near and want you to know they are happy and well. Taking the word loss out of your vocabulary when referring to the passing of a loved one will help tremendously. Instead of saying, "I lost my loved one."—which isn't true, you could say, "My son passed...," or "My father made his transition...," Referring to loss doesn't feel good because it is not true. Any time you speak something that is not true, you don't feel good.

Our Loved Ones Are With Us—Your loved ones are with you, and if you relax a bit and ask for help to feel their presence, you will—if you believe it is possible. Just think of them, think their name, and they can be with you. Even if you can't feel them just yet, trust they are there, and ask them to help you or give you a sign. Your part in this is to pay attention, and when you receive a sign accept it with appreciation. Try not to question it or make an excuse why it is probably a fluke.

Our Loved Ones Are Happy—Everyone wants to know their loved ones are OK. Your loved ones are more than OK. They are happy and feel immense love. When your loved ones transitioned, all the resistance they carried was released. Can you even imagine what it must feel like to have all fear immediately released? They also experience love that we cannot comprehend while in our human bodies. Your loved ones in the nonphysical are doing much better than they were in their bodies. They want you to know that you, too, can feel better now, so please don't worry about them—no matter the circumstances of their life or their passing.

Our Connection of Love is Never Broken—This is one of the best surprises I have experienced since Garrett transitioned. I did not expect our relationship and love to continue to build and deepen, but it did. To my great joy, I feel a continued close connection that grows deeper with time, just as it was when he was in his body. It's hard to explain how this could be if you didn't know there is no death.

We Choose Our Parents—Years ago I heard that we choose our parents, and at the time it seemed like a farfetched idea. I just could not imagine that we chose our parents before being born. As I grew and opened up to new ways of thinking, I found more evidence that this may be true. Many spiritual teachers share that we do choose our parents before being born. Many think, Why would I have chosen this? We choose from a spiritual perspective based on what our Soul wants to learn, and every situation is perfect from the Soul perspective. I feel the bond with my sons. I know that we chose to be mother and sons together for our spiritual growth. I also know that they chose their fathers for the same reason.

Our Loved Ones Will Help Us—Even if you cannot hear your loved ones in the nonphysical, they can hear you. They know how you're feeling, and they understand you completely. You can ask them for help about anything. You can also ask your guardian angels for help as well. Because of free will, they cannot help unless invited to do so. You can speak out loud or in your head; they will hear you. Ask for a sign. They will help you in ways you may not know. I have found that I could sense when Garrett has had his hand in something. You will, too.

I Can Choose Peace Over Pain and Sorrow—Try to embrace this. It is the most empowering thing you can do for yourself. I had learned the concept of choosing peace years before Garrett passed. It had worked for me when I was being challenged by Garrett as a teenager. It works in any situation. We always have a choice on how we feel. I remember making the conscious choice to allow myself to grieve, to accept, and feel better that Garrett had transitioned. Sometimes all I could say was I can choose this or peace as a mantra. I could get myself in a peaceful place. Then, there might be something that would remind me of Garrett, like Ranch dressing on a menu, and I would well up in tears because it would remind me that he put Ranch dressing on everything—and now he's not here. I would allow the moment and then remind myself that he *is* here, and I do not have to feel badly. I can change my response from sadness that he is no longer in his body to a smile and a chuckle. I would remember how I couldn't believe he dipped his pizza in Ranch dressing or put it on his eggs. It's a practice in consciousness, paying attention to how I responded and how I wanted to respond. It takes time.

I still remind myself when I start to get annoyed by a situation or someone that I can choose to feel peace and love, or I can choose to be angry. Because feeling good and not carrying anger within me is important to me, my well-being is number one. I am getting much better at this.

I Am Much More Than I Thought—Before Garrett's transition, I never gave much thought about what happens when we pass. I was interested in spirituality and a better way of being in the world. Even though I had felt and communicated with my dad and grandfather after they passed, I never pursued what happens or where we are when we leave our bodies. Now that this subject had my attention, I have become present and conscious to so much more about who we really are, that we are spiritual beings having a physical experience. We have a Higher Self, a Soul, whatever you want to call it, that is wise. And we can each tap in to it while we are in a body. It's that intuitive sense we all have. How in tune we are to it is how well we hear it. When in nonphysical, we are multidimensional.

Since I have little concept of what it is like to be in nonphysical, it's hard to understand fully what it is, and I don't think we can comprehend it while we're in a body, nor do I think we are meant to. I have a sense that it is more than transitioning and going to heaven and hanging out with God and angels. There is a life force that runs through all of us, that we all can connect with, and it's the source of love that is our natural state of being. This is what I believe our loved ones in nonphysical want us to know. There is only love, and fear is something that we have brought into the mix.

I Can Directly Communicate with Those in Nonphysical Form—It is fun to know when I think of or am reminded of something by Garrett, that he is right with me in that moment. I know that he is the one who brought the thought. It's the same as if he was in his body and using his voice to tell me. When Garrett and I had talked about communicating through telepathy, it is the same thing. He is communicating with me very clearly. Sometimes, I'll just feel his presence or see him, and it is the same as if he just stopped by—because he has. If I've forgotten something, he reminds me. He makes his presence known to both me and his brother on a daily basis. He makes me laugh. The other day I felt him flick the back of my head in a playful way. I mentioned it to my son Ryan, and he said Garrett did the same thing to him earlier in the day. Garrett's sense of humor and playfulness comes through to us often. There have been times when I can feel Garrett's love for me, and it is so strong that it brings me to tears. The amount of love can be overwhelming.

Initially, my experience connecting with those in nonphysical was with family members. After embracing my multi-senses, my connection expanded to those in nonphysical whom I have never met in physical form.

Our Culture Promotes Victimization and Loss—As I was grieving, I was noticing things that people said that made me feel better—and also things that made me feel worse. So much of our language around the passing of a loved one, especially young people, is victimizing. I believe the language used around transitioning is detrimental to our well-being and counters the truth of the matter. Words uplift or they do not; it is that simple. If words are not uplifting, then they are not of love. Untimely passing is a term I hear often when anyone who is not elderly passes, but who says it is untimely? The person's Soul would consider it the perfect time, Divine time.

We Are Safe—Our fear, especially as parents, centers on safety. The fact is, we are always safe; nothing can go wrong. When you begin to look at life from this perspective, you can be happier, easier about life. I'm not talking about letting go of common sense. I am, however, referring to things that seem random. There are no random events or flukes because everything unfolds the way it's supposed to. Your Soul directs events that are for your highest good. It may not seem like you are always safe from your physical perspective, so it is important to remember there is a broader perspective. As you begin to see life from a spiritual perspective, the broader perspective will show you the perfection in everything. Since there is no death, only more life, there is nothing to fear. There is no end—only more. More growth, more learning, more fun. No matter what happens, there is a choice in the way events are perceived—either from a place of love or a place of fear. The choice you make is the place you choose to live.

Spiritual Perspective Transforms Grief—I grew up believing life was hard and in my twenties did not have much fun, but I gained new perspectives that allowed me to see life is supposed to be fun. It does not have to be hard. Life begins to get easy, or easier, when you believe it is possible to be easy, and then you can really stretch yourself in some cases and choose to believe it is easy and see how things shift for you. I have changed my thinking on so many topics, but there are still more I can change. It's fun discovering another place I can grow and let go. Having been able to do this with Garrett's transition has become my benchmark. If I can be at peace, happy, and connected with him since he has passed, I know I can achieve anything. This was by far the highest mountain to climb; it was my Everest.

There Are No Untimely Passings—How can anyone possibly know that someone's passing is untimely? This is only an opinion, a judgment, and an arrogance. The challenge is this: our culture has bought into this thinking, and it has created more pain for the loved ones processing the grief. Plus, it is not true. It is the viewpoint that something has gone wrong when in fact nothing can go wrong. The Divine does not make mistakes. Every Soul chooses the time to transition, and it is always the perfect time for the Soul to exit the body. It is challenging enough processing the fact that your loved one has transitioned. Thinking it is wrong in some way only digs in and makes the grief and coming to terms with it all the more difficult to process. Think about it. If you knew that your loved one transitioned in the exact moment he or she was supposed to, would that not alleviate your pain? Knowing everything happened exactly as planned, and knowing they are happy, wouldn't you begin to look at passing differently?

My Beliefs And Thinking Control The Way I Feel—Before Garrett's passing, I knew that my beliefs, which are my thoughts, control how I feel. And that I could choose to change them. I had practiced this in choosing peace during challenging times in my life, never thinking that I would experience the passing of a child and try to use them in that situation. It did happen. My son did transition. I was ready to begin to challenge the beliefs I had about death, and this began to turn my pain around. Thought by thought, I began the practice of changing my beliefs. Every time I noticed that I was thinking a negative thought, I asked myself, "What do I really believe about this?" Gradually, it became easier to remember what I believe, what I knew to be true. Another thing that helped was my awareness of others. I stayed away from those who tended to make me feel worse when I was around them. They were well-meaning people, but they were coming from fear, and I was in the process of moving from old, fearful thoughts to a place of love.

Spiritual Awakening and Growth—When a loved one passes, remember that you have a deep capacity for love, and you also are given an opportunity for a spiritual awakening. You get to choose how you want to be, what you want to learn, and how you want to feel. If you have the desire to feel better and to understand what is here for you as a result of this event, know that you can and will. If you turn to your own spirituality for answers, to find the relief of feeling at peace, you will have embraced an opportunity that forever changes your life and your perspective of life—physical and nonphysical. There is no other way than through your own experience. You can't read about it; you have to experience the event and move through it.

Chapter Twenty-Seven

Transformation and Peace

Each one of us has to find his peace from within.
And peace to be real must be unaffected by outside circumstances.
— *Mahatma Gandhi*

There is something much deeper that calls us all. Sometimes we hear the calling and ignore it, but sometimes we hear and follow. Although I was heeding my spiritual calling, for years constantly studying and beginning a spiritual practice, it wasn't until Garrett transitioned that I completely surrendered. It was the catalyst that propelled me to depths I would not have known had I not experienced his transition.

After Garrett transitioned I would wake up hoping it was a bad dream and scream in agony over the fact that my son was not in his body. It was unbearable. I was doubtful I would ever be happy or feel joy again. Reflecting on my life and experiences, I can see how all roads led me to my place of peace with Garrett. It was an opportunity to look at everything and clear out those things that no longer served me.

The learning is that we are Consciousness, not bodies, and that there is much more going on than most of us realize. I don't think it's possible for us, while in our human bodies, to comprehend everything we're not supposed to know. We are meant to wake up, to understand that we are spiritual beings, and to know that we have access to our loved ones in the nonphysical. We are also here to remember that we are spiritual beings. Everything in this life experience is spiritual. There is nothing to fear; we are always safe; and we are always loved. We *are* love. Our normal state is at the multi-sensory level. We all have these gifts, and we use them every day, knowingly or unknowingly.

The landscape of my world has changed tremendously since Garrett transitioned. He hasn't died. I still stay in constant contact with him. Our relationships are eternal and based in love. There is only love. It is in our humanness that we bring in fear and judgment. The Life Force within us guides us with our intuition, gut feelings, or whatever else you want to call it. It's here within where we should be living our lives, not outside ourselves. The awakening comes from within. No one else knows better for you than you. We've been trained to look outside ourselves, to believe things that are contrary to our own knowing. The challenge is to be present and trust. Intuition is subtle, but fear and outside opinions are loud.

When you hear the truth, you know it because it resonates within, and you can feel it. It's time to quit doubting your own knowing because of what you've been told. It's time to listen to your Higher Self, your guidance. Be centered in love rather than in fear. It is in this place you'll know your truths, you'll have a knowing. You'll sense, see, or hear your loved one and trust your knowing. It's time to begin operating from your heart rather than your head. Inner guidance isn't always logical, but it's always right. How many times have you said, "I knew that"? Start trusting it.

When you choose to accept that all is well, you will know that nothing has gone wrong. There are no Divine mistakes or accidents. Our loved ones have chosen to leave at a certain day and time. It changes everything. If I grieve now, I know it's because for a moment I've forgotten what I know, that my loved one is here and well. When you begin to see the perfection in everything, then you see the world in a completely new light. The only way this can happen is to look at it from a spiritual point of view.

We can be taught a belief, such as we go to heaven when we die. And then there is a knowing that resonates deep within oneself, and that is what transformed within me. I knew things that I had read and been taught, but it wasn't until I felt them in my heart, until I had a resonance with them, that I felt peace. We can feel this if we choose this peace over all else.

During the first year of Garrett's transition I realized how much I wanted peace in my heart. There was overwhelming turmoil in my life. I had to surrender. I wanted peace in every area of my life. It's easy to see that how I was feeling on the inside was reflected on the outside.

When you invite peace into your life, your way of being changes. You're more centered and calm. You respond to life's challenges with more ease and trust. Peace is an inner knowing that all is well.

Garrett loves peace. During his teenage years, there was always something in him that craved peace. When it was achieved, he would light up, literally from the inside out. When he transitioned, I have no doubt he was in a place of complete peace. He wanted to share it with everyone with whom he came in contact. He wanted others to feel and know what he had learned. I am certain that Garrett wants everyone to know peace.

Message from Garrett

Thank you to everyone who helped my mom after my transition. She's strong and brave, but you made all the difference for her. While I'm in nonphysical and could help, she needed all of us to get where she is right now. Because of your love and support, she can help others who have been in, or are in, her shoes. We are here to love and help each other discover the peace within each of us and share this love with others. When we do this, we are doing what we have come to learn. There is no separation. When one hurts, we all hurt. When one is healed, we all benefit. Blessings and peace to all. The drama created can be quite amusing. We're not laughing at you, but you all can be quite amusing.

With love and respect,

Garrett.

About the Author

After a divorce and years of feeling professionally unfulfilled in the corporate world, Dana switched gears and changed her career. She heeded her Soul's longing for something more. This led Dana to obtain her coaching credentials so that she could begin a career and a leadership development coaching practice.

Soon after this career change, her nineteen-year-old son Garrett was hit by a train, and Dana's life took a dramatic turn. This event brought Dana to her knees as she found herself in the midst of the most unbearable pain she could imagine. Garrett's passing caused Dana to question everything she had learned about life. These questions gave way to answers and new understandings that changed every part of her being. While grieving for her son, Dana discovered that her connection with him did not end with his leaving his physical body.

Taking all she had learned from this profound experience, Dana created a broader, more in-depth approach to her work. Combining powerful, intuitive coaching skills with a spiritual perspective, she provides a unique and dynamic platform for her clients.

As an adjunct faculty member at Marylhurst University in Lake Oswego, Oregon, Dana has collaboratively pioneered the development and instruction of a series of highly successful coaching and leadership classes. Participants in these courses are adult students and professionals wanting to learn, build and strengthen their coaching and leadership skills.

Prior to establishing her coaching practice, Dana Smith was a managing partner of a thriving sales and marketing consulting company. Her extensive professional career experience in sales, marketing, and public relations spans start-ups to Fortune 500 companies in the high-technology industry. Dana is a co-founder and board chair of Garrett's Space, a nonprofit organization supporting young people.

Website: www.danasmithllc.com

Garrett's Space

Garrett's Space is the vision and dream of Garrett Kyle, who recognized the need in the community for a place dedicated to serving young people. Garrett's Space offers a coffee and juice bar with games—a place for high school and college-age students to "kick it." But it is much more than this. We intend to provide an entire resource center with computers; support for resume writing and interview skills; job resources; school information; and opportunities to discover individual gifts and talents. The focus is to support the well-being of young people by providing them with the tools they need to become successful, happy adults who contribute their gifts and talents to the world.

Part of the proceeds of this book will support building Garrett's dream.

Website: www.garrettspace.org

Resources

Ask and It Is Given: Learning to Manifest Your Desires, by Esther and Jerry Hicks

Sacred Contracts, by Caroline Myss

Simple Abundance: A Daybook of Comfort and Joy, by Sarah Ban Breathnach

The Alchemist, by Paulo Coelho

The Power of Now, by Eckhart Tolle

There's a Spiritual Solution to Every Problem, by Wayne Dyer

If you're interested in angels, any book by Doreen Virtue.

Made in the USA
Lexington, KY
25 November 2013